YORK NOTES

General Editors: Professor A.N. Jeffares (*University of Stirling*) & Professor Suheil Bushrui (*American University of Beirut*)

Harold Brighouse

HOBSON'S CHOICE

Notes by John Goodby

BA (HULL), MA, PH D (LEEDS)
Tutor of English, Harrogate Tutorial College

LONGMAN
YORK PRESS

YORK PRESS
Immeuble Esseily, Place Riad Solh, Beirut.

LONGMAN GROUP UK LIMITED
Longman House,
Burnt Mill,
Harlow,
Essex

First published in 1988

ISBN 0-582-02096-4

Produced by Longman Group (FE) Ltd
Typeset by Boldface Typesetters, London EC1
Printed in Hong Kong

Contents

Part 1

Introduction

ALTHOUGH he was a prolific and popular playwright and novelist during his lifetime, the reputation of Harold Brighouse today rests almost entirely on his play *Hobson's Choice*. Over seventy years after its first performance, Brighouse's masterpiece remains one of the most frequently performed of twentieth-century English plays. This is because, like its author, *Hobson's Choice* is representative of all that was best in the Manchester School of dramatists and the golden age of the Repertory Movement.

The life of Harold Brighouse

1882-1899

Harold Brighouse was born in Eccles near Salford on 26 July 1882. A year before, his father John Southworth Brighouse had sinned against Victorian propriety by marrying his late wife's sister, and both Harold and his sister Hilda (born in 1884) were technically illegitimate until a change in the law some twenty years later. Memories of his parents' defiance of convention would prompt Brighouse to pay them a tribute in *Hobson's Choice*, in which Maggie and Will Mossop are married in 1880—the year in which his parents had decided to marry.

The Brighouse family, however, was no more literary or theatrical than the average middle-class family of the day. Indeed, Brighouse's father could be intolerant of literature. On one occasion, having been persuaded by a review to buy a copy of *Esther Waters* (a new novel by the Irish writer George Moore (1852–1933)), he had thrown it, half-read, into the fire. 'That,' his son was to comment in his autobiography, 'from a respecter of books and property, was a memorable gesture.' John Brighouse was a manager in the cotton-spinning industry and Treasurer of the Eccles Liberal Institute, a man with a seemingly secure future. Behind the prosperous appearance, however, things were somewhat different. Out of a sense of family duty, John Brighouse often helped his five brothers-in-law with loans, many of which were never repaid. His later discovery of how near his father had been to ruin may have influenced Brighouse's handling of the threat to Hobson's business in his most famous play. But, looking back,

Brighouse saw that his childhood had been a happy one: 'We were Late Victorians. It was a thriving, broadcloth age. The British Navy, policing the world, guaranteed progress.'

If the family had no interest in the theatre there was nevertheless an academic model in the family for the young Harold Brighouse. His mother's brother, Edwin Harrison, had been a prodigy in Classics who had been awarded a scholarship to Oxford, where he had excelled in examinations and impressed his fellow-students with his wit and insight. His frailty had, however, prevented him from realising his potential, and he had died young. This was a tragedy for which Mrs Brighouse wished to compensate by making a success of her own son. But although he won a scholarship to Manchester Grammar School, Harold was no Classics genius. Perhaps as a result of undue academic pressure, he decided to follow in his father's rather than his uncle's footsteps when he left school. At the age of seventeen he decided to start work in the cotton industry rather than go up to the University of Oxford.

1899–1909

Brighouse entered a shipping merchant's office and worked as a trainee textile buyer at ten shillings (50p) a week. At this point in his career he still had no interest in the theatre; 'Where, then, did the theatre come in?' he asks himself in his autobiography, and answers, 'Effectively, nowhere.' But during his lunch-breaks at work, Brighouse began passing his time by walking around Manchester city centre. Near his workplace he discovered no fewer than ten music-halls and theatres. They provided a form of escape from his job, and at one of them, the Royal, Brighouse attended a season of plays in the summer of 1900. From that time on he was obsessed by the theatre.

Despite his Northern origins it was the impact of London which did most to further Brighouse's ambition to be a dramatist himself. In 1902 his company allowed him to go to London to help to set up their new office there. With his evenings free for theatre-going, he became a regular attender of 'first nights', the first performances of new plays at various theatres in the West End. It was as a 'gallery first-nighter' that he met Emily Lynes, who worked as an assistant to a leading society photographer. Not long afterwards they became engaged, and returned to Withington in Manchester where they were married. Brighouse had already obtained a promise from his company that they would allow him to deal with their business in London. His main motive for this was to keep up with new plays in the capital, and he maintained his season ticket as before.

Brighouse had been promoted and was now earning £150 a year. But theatre-going had made him dissatisfied with his work, which he now regarded as a 'blind-alley occupation'. Then, in 1908, on one of his frequent visits to London, he saw a play that he described as so 'outrageously bad' that he determined to write a better one. In accordance with the prevailing taste of the time he wrote a five-act romantic drama and sent it off to the actor-manager J. Forbes-Robertson (1853–1937) who was then in Manchester with his touring company. The play was rejected, but Forbes-Robertson advised Brighouse to 'try one-acters — write of the life you know'. One-act plays were very common at this period, and were used as curtain-raisers before the main play was performed. The suggestion was inspired; Brighouse immediately wrote his first and best one-act play, *Lonesome-like*. It was accepted at once by the Gaiety Theatre in Manchester, although it was not staged until two years later, in 1911, when it ran for over three thousand performances.

1909–1915

Although Brighouse had become a textile salesman, and could claim that his attitude to play-writing 'fell short of fanaticism', he was devoting all his spare time to writing. He would sometimes wake at 3 a.m. to write before he went to work; his aim was to break away from the textile trade. He told a friend that 'the theatre was the only way out for me'.

The first play by Brighouse to be produced was another one-acter, *The Doorway*, which was staged in 1909 at the Gaiety Theatre in Manchester. His mother, dying of cancer, saw in his success a fulfilment of her dreams for her son. A year later Brighouse's first full-length play, *Dealing in Futures*, was produced at another of the repertory theatres, in Glasgow. From this promising beginning he never looked back. After the First World War he was able to give up working in textiles and concentrate on his writing. His output eventually totalled fifty one-act and fifteen full-length plays, in addition to eight novels. He also contributed over one hundred articles to *The Manchester Guardian* and was, for a while, one of its drama critics.

Much of Brighouse's success was paralleled by the rise of what was known as the Repertory Movement which, from 1907 onwards, saw the spread of serious drama to the major British cities outside London and the formation of professional theatre companies there. It had begun with the famous seasons of plays presented between 1904 and 1907 at the Court Theatre in London under the management of Harley Granville-Barker (1877–1946) and J.E. Vedrenne (1867–1930). When the Court Theatre season ended, enthusiasts transferred its experimental repertory to the provinces. Brighouse had been influenced by his attendance at the early productions at the Court Theatre, and his career was largely the result of the Repertory Movement. Repertory had been brought to Manchester by Miss A.E. Horniman (1860–1937), who had bought the Gaiety Theatre, and whose sponsorship of Lancashire drama helped to give rise to the Manchester School of playwrights between 1909 and 1914.

The three most outstanding members of the Manchester School were Stanley Houghton (1881–1913), the author of *Hindle Wakes* (1911), Allan Monkhouse (1858–1936) and Brighouse himself. Their plays were distinguished by the use of working-class and middle-class characters in a Lancashire setting, using Lancashire dialect. This was in contrast to the majority of plays produced in London which were usually based on the lives of the upper and upper-middle classes. Brighouse and his fellow-playwrights saw it as part of their job to show that the lives of working people in the industrial North could be as fit a subject for drama as those of members of polite London society. Occasionally Brighouse admitted to feeling aggrieved at the indifference of London audiences to the sort of plays which were produced by dramatists like himself. 'Only by exceptional merit . . . can a regional play overcome London's Mayfair prejudice,' he wrote in his autobiography. Yet for all that he wanted acceptance and success in London. With *Hobson's Choice* he was to achieve it.

Brighouse and *Hobson's Choice*

Hobson's Choice: its writing

Although *Hobson's Choice* was written over seventy years ago, the full story behind Brighouse's reasons for writing it has only recently come to light through the researches of Dr Paul Mortimer. At the outbreak of the First World War, Brighouse was in France. In the previous year, 1913, his friend and fellow Manchester School playwright Stanley Houghton had fallen ill in Venice and was taken back to Manchester where he died four months later. Brighouse had put together a memorial edition of Houghton's plays, and, whilst compiling the book, had discovered a notebook in which Houghton had listed the titles of projected plays. One of these was *Hobson's Choice*. Brighouse remembered that five years earlier he and Houghton had met Iden Payne, the director of the Gaiety Theatre, in the bar of the Midland Hotel in Manchester. During their meeting Payne had mentioned that a play by Monkhouse, recently staged at the Gaiety, had done badly because of the weak cast he had chosen. When Brighouse and Houghton asked Payne why he had hired such bad actors, he had replied, 'It was Hobson's Choice. No others were available.' Both playwrights had been struck by the potential the proverbial phrase might have as a play title, and both had claimed it. In order to resolve the issue Payne had flipped a coin; and it had been Houghton, not Brighouse, who had won the toss.

When war broke out in France in 1914, Brighouse made his way to the Channel on a bus driven by a conscript. The other passengers were women who had been weeping all day. The emotional reactions to the impending historical tragedy combined in Brighouse's mind with the memory of his dead friend to provide the impetus for a new play. It was to take place in the year 1880 because that had been the year in which his parents had decided upon their unorthodox marriage. It was to be set in the very cobbler's shop on Gilda Brook Road, Eccles, to which his mother had taken him as a child to buy his boots. Even the cellar trap-door of the place would be duplicated exactly. The character of Maggie was to be drawn from that of his sister Hilda, down to her exact age at the time the play was being written. It was as if, in the face of massive hostilities and destruction, Brighouse wished to write a play which would represent all that was most admirable and humane in the Lancashire character. Finally, the title of the play itself would represent a tribute to his late friend. As soon as he arrived back from France, Brighouse started work on his new play.

Hobson's Choice: its first production

By 1915 Brighouse had finished the play, but he found that London's war-time producers were not keen on staging it. Nor was he enthusiastic about a first production in London. The war atmosphere meant that serious and subtle drama would have great difficulty in finding a good audience. The theatres were full of troops on leave with their girlfriends, and their taste was for light revue and the music-hall. The same problems were faced by other dramatists of the time; one of Shaw's greatest plays, *Heartbreak House* (written 1916–17), could not be produced until after the war. So, in order to have his play produced under better conditions, Brighouse sent it to Iden Payne, then in New York. Payne agreed to produce the play. Although *Hobson's Choice* did not fare very well when it was tried out on tour, the opening at the Princess Theatre, New York, on 23 November 1915 was a great success. With this behind it, the first London production took place on 22 June 1916 at the Apollo Theatre where it proved to be extremely popular, and grossed the equivalent of twenty thousand pounds in one week. It ran for 246 performances there and, later, at the Prince of Wales Theatre.

Hobson's Choice and censorship

Brighouse's masterpiece came close to not being shown at all because of the stringent censorship laws then in force in Britain. The main obstacle was the end of Act III, where Maggie leads Will by the ear to the bedroom. 'The Censorship of 1916', Brighouse commented, 'boggled at this scene.' He had had trouble before when the word 'bloody', allowed in Shaw's *Pygmalion* (1912), was deleted from his own play *Garside's Career* in 1914. It was stipulated, after much persuasion, that the scene could only be retained if there were no complaints from the public during the first few days of performance. One single objection would have led to the deletion of the scene. The attitude of officialdom to the play as a whole is revealed by the fact that when it was submitted to the Lord Chamberlain for licence, his office recorded that it was 'a study of rather disagreeable provincial folk'.

Hobson's Choice: later history

Hobson's Choice was published in 1916, and has been staged almost continuously by amateur and professional theatre groups ever since. It has also been a success in several adapted forms. Brighouse rewrote the play as a novel in 1917, by which time it was so well known that it could be titled simply *Hobson's*. In 1954 it was made into a film starring Charles Laughton as Henry Hobson, John Mills as Will Mossop and Brenda de Banzie as Maggie Hobson. Although he had nothing to do with the making of the film, and was privately unhappy about the script, Brighouse issued a press release at the time supporting it. The film went on to win the British Academy Award for the Best Film of 1954. In addition, *Hobson's Choice* has been broadcast many times on radio and television, and was even turned into a Broadway musical in 1966. The last major London revival of the play took place in February 1982 at the Theatre Royal, the cast including Penelope Keith, Anthony Quayle and Trevor Peacock.

1915–1958

At the beginning of the First World War Brighouse was rejected by the Army as unfit for active service, but in 1917 he was made a propaganda writer for Military Intelligence in the newly formed Royal Air Force. When the war ended in 1918 he continued to consolidate his position as the most successful playwright of the Manchester School. He produced a steady stream of plays of various types, including *The Northerners*, *Zack* and *The Game* which were published as *Three Lancashire Plays*. The last of these was made into a film, as was *The Winning Goal*. A further Lancashire trilogy appeared in the 1920s, along with plays written for outdoor performance. Brighouse had some popular success as a novelist too; an adaptation of Houghton's play *Hindle Wakes* sold half-a-million copies.

In 1930, for reasons which are not yet clear, Brighouse virtually stopped writing. By this time, however, his financial position was secure. His joint income from plays, fiction, and literary work for *The Manchester Guardian* probably enabled him to live by his writing from 1914 onwards. After the success of *Hobson's Choice*, the cotton firm of which his father was Managing Director made Harold a Director. He generally turned up for the monthly Board meetings; and when John Southworth Brighouse died in 1917 he left Harold and Hilda £15,000 in his will. Despite being a poor manager of his financial affairs, Brighouse was able to maintain himself comfortably enough after giving up writing. During a tour of Canada and the U.S.A. offers were made to him to turn his plays into films, but apart from the three plays mentioned, these offers were turned down.

By nature Brighouse was a quiet, reserved person who shunned publicity. He spent most of his time either alone or with his few friends, and his sister recalled how he would retreat into the attic on the occasions when visitors called. Towards the end of his life he insisted that, on his death, all of his papers should be burnt. Although he had written nothing but a few newspaper articles for almost thirty years, Brighouse continued to attend plays and was making notes for new plays of his own at the time of his death in London in 1958.

The title

The saying 'Hobson's Choice' is proverbial, having passed into common usage from the practices of one Thomas Hobson (?1544–1631), a Cambridge livery stables owner and waggoner. At his stable the customers had no choice of horse but the next one available, and hence no choice at all.

A note on the text

Hobson's Choice was published and copyrighted in 1916 by Samuel French Ltd., London, with whom Brighouse worked as Drama Adviser. Today the play is published by Heinemann Educational Books, London, in a Hereford Plays edition with an Introduction (1964) by E.R. Wood. This paperback edition has been used in the preparation of these notes.

Part 2

Summaries
of HOBSON'S CHOICE

A general summary

Act I

Act I takes place in Hobson's Boot Shop in Salford in the year 1880. Hobson's daughters are discussing their father, who has risen late. Alice's suitor, Albert Prosser, enters the shop, but before he can start talking to Alice, Maggie, the oldest sister, intercepts him and forces him to buy a pair of boots. She then shows him out of the shop. Hobson enters to say that he is going out. Maggie, Alice and Vickey warn him not to be late for dinner; they believe he is going to the Moonraker's Inn to drink. Hobson rebukes them for their bumptiousness. He announces his intention to marry them off to husbands of his own choosing in order to be rid of them, although he makes an exception of Maggie whom he regards as an old maid.

As he is about to leave, the wealthy Mrs Hepworth enters the shop. Hobson is so obsequious towards her that she says he looks ridiculous. She wishes to know who made a pair of boots that she bought from the shop. Hobson thinks that she wants to complain about them and he promises to punish the workman responsible. But Mrs Hepworth thinks the boots are the best-made pair she has ever had, and she leaves her calling card with Will Mossop, the workman who made them. After telling Will to let her know if he ever leaves Hobson's, she goes out.

Jim Heeler, a friend of Hobson's, now enters to take Hobson with him to the Moonraker's. Before he can do so, Hobson sends his daughters out so that he can discuss with Jim the problems he is having with them. He mentions his idea of marrying Alice and Vickey off, but when Jim says that, as their father, he will have to provide them with dowries, he changes his mind. He does not pay his daughters wages anyway, he adds, and he and Jim leave the shop together.

Maggie re-enters, and calls up Will Mossop again from the cellar. She is determined to marry him, but Will does not understand at first what she wants. He thinks Maggie is simply proposing a business relationship; as the truth dawns on him he protests, saying that he is not ambitious and is already engaged to Ada Figgins, his landlady's daughter. This does not deter Maggie, and when Ada comes in with Will's lunch she argues with her about who should have Will. Ada is completely overwhelmed, but as she leaves she threatens Will with the wrath of her mother when he returns that evening. Maggie arranges for Will to change lodgings, and when her sisters come in she tells them about the marriage. They are both shocked. Hobson now returns from the Moonraker's, and when Maggie tells him what she has done and proposes that he starts to pay her wages, he loses his temper. Calling Will up from the cellar workshop, he begins to beat him for wanting to marry Maggie, despite Will's protests that he does not. But Hobson's blow rouses Will to opposition and he kisses her, declaring that he will set up with Maggie if Hobson touches him again. Maggie is delighted.

Act II

It is a month later in Hobson's Boot Shop. Maggie and Will have already left, and Alice and Vickey are looking after the shop. They are, however, incapable of running things and do not know what orders to give to Tubby, the remaining workman. They mention that Hobson is now spending more time than ever at the Moonraker's. Maggie and Will enter with Freddy Beenstock, Vickey's suitor. The younger sisters complain that Hobson refuses to let them go out since Maggie and Will left. They think it will be impossible for them to get married. Freddy tells them that their father, on his way home from the Moonraker's, has fallen through the trapdoor of Beenstock's corn warehouse and is now sleeping there. Maggie sends Freddy off to fetch Albert with a legal document that Maggie has asked him to draw up for her. She informs Alice and Vickey that in future they must treat Will with more respect because he has his own business. By way of recognising this they agree, under protest, to kiss him. Maggie then reveals that she and Will are being married that afternoon, and that Vickey, Alice, Freddy and Albert are to attend.

Much to the consternation of her sisters, Maggie now selects a four-penny brass ring from the shop's stock to serve as a wedding ring. Will is then sent upstairs for some broken furniture. Although it is of no use to Vickey or Alice, they are rather reluctant to let it go. However, Maggie over-rides their objections by announcing that she has a plan for getting them both marriage-settlements. When Freddy and Albert enter, Maggie puts Freddy to work helping Will and reads from the legal document Albert has brought. It is an action for trespass and damages against her father by Beenstock's Corn Merchants. Freddy is told to take it and pin it to Hobson while he is asleep. While the girls are getting ready for the wedding, Albert is persuaded to take the loaded handcart round to Maggie's and Will's home. Tubby is left in charge of the shop as the girls re-enter and everyone sets off for the wedding.

Act III

The third act is set in the living-room-cum-workshop in the cellar on Old-field Road. Maggie and Will have just been married, and the guests are toasting the bride and groom. Will makes a speech of thanks, and his fluency surprises Alice and Vickey. Maggie says she is educating him, and adds that in twenty years' time she thinks Will will be better off than either Albert or Freddy. The guests are baffled about the source of the money for Will's business. Will then starts to clear up the table, and when Albert and Freddy laugh at him, Maggie orders them to help him. She takes Alice and Vickey into the bedroom for a chat; left to themselves, the men do the clearing and washing up. Will tells them that he is worried about being left alone with Maggie, and asks them to stay longer. Maggie and the girls come back into the room; and now there is a knock at the door. It is Hobson. The girls, Albert and Freddy hide in the bedroom. Maggie makes a show of asking Will whether she can let her father in; when he agrees, she makes Hobson shake hands with her husband and eat a slice of wedding-cake to show his acceptance of her marriage.

Hobson has come to Maggie for advice. She agrees to give it, but only if Will is allowed to stay. Hobson then explains that he is ruined; news of his drunken accident will reach the ears of his respectable customers when the case comes to court, and they will refuse to patronise his shop. With prompting by Maggie, he agrees that it would be better if he could settle out of court, although not in a lawyer's office. At this point Maggie tells him that Albert is in the other room, and he and the others come out of hiding. Albert proposes a settlement of a thousand pounds, but even Maggie thinks this is too much. They settle on five hundred, and Hobson gives his word as a bond in front of witnesses. Now he is told that the money will really be used as wedding settlements for Vickey and Alice. He is furious at having been tricked and storms out. The guests leave after Hobson, leaving Will and Maggie together. Maggie gives Will a brief writing exercise to copy out and goes to bed. When he has finished it, Will lies down to sleep on the couch. But Maggie comes in once again, takes Will by the ear, and leads him into the bedroom.

Act IV

The last act is set in Hobson's living-room next door to his shop. It is a year after the marriage of Maggie and Will. The room is neglected and dirty. Tubby is ineptly making breakfast for Hobson, who has said that he is very ill, but is, nevertheless, getting up. Jim Heeler enters. Tubby tells him that a doctor has already been sent for, and goes on to say that Hobson's business is being ruined by his temper. At this point Hobson himself appears, unshaved and collarless. Tubby, worried by his appearance, hurries off to summon Hobson's daughters. Jim listens as Hobson relates how he could not wash or shave because he was afraid he might kill himself. They both wonder whether drinking might possibly be the cause of Hobson's problem. Doctor MacFarlane enters. He dismisses Jim and, after looking at Hobson, diagnoses him as a chronic alcoholic. He makes out a prescription for him, although Hobson swears he will not give up drink. The doctor is angry at Hobson's obstinacy; he asks whether he has any female relatives who might be able to look after him. Hobson's account of his daughters' 'uppishness' convinces the doctor that Maggie is the only person who can save him from drinking himself to death, and he orders Hobson to get Maggie back. Maggie now enters, having received Tubby's message, and before the doctor leaves she promises him that she will consider his arguments.

Hobson takes it for granted that Maggie would be prepared to do what the doctor suggests. When she says she must consult Will first, Hobson scoffs at the idea. Alice and Vickey enter; but when they are told what the situation is, they both say it is Maggie's duty to look after their father and give excuses why they cannot do it. They, too, mock Maggie's insistence on consulting Will first. But Will is by now already in the shop next door looking over the stock. Alice and Vickey are shocked by his presumption; when Maggie goes off to talk with Will, they reveal that they are afraid that Hobson might favour Maggie and Will above them in his will. Maggie and Will now return from the shop. While Maggie goes to find Hobson, who has gone to put a collar on, Will and her sisters argue. Will stands up to them both. He makes it clear he would only agree to let Maggie look after Hobson if he himself moved in too; and this he will only do on his own terms. Hobson and Maggie re-enter, and Hobson asks Alice and Vickey in turn whether they are prepared to move in to look after him. They refuse, and Hobson sends them home. He then proposes to Maggie that she look after him, and that he employ Will again on his old wage. They reject this completely, for their own business is doing well.

Will now puts his proposals to Hobson. He must make Will an equal partner in his business, must not interfere with the business, and must also allow its name to be changed to 'Mossop and Hobson'. Hobson has no choice; the meaning of the title of the play becomes clear. He is beaten, and goes off to get ready to see a lawyer who will draw up the partnership deeds. Maggie and Will exchange endearments in his absence, and Maggie refuses Will's offer to replace her brass ring with a real gold one. The play ends with Will's incredulous exclamation at the reversals of fortune that have taken place: 'Well, by gum!'

Detailed summaries

Act I

Brighouse's stage directions for Act I are very detailed, and give us information about the situation in Hobson's shop before any dialogue is spoken. We are told that the shop is 'dingy but business-like'; that it is 'prosperous', but that this does not mean very much because it was not necessary to equip a business elaborately in order to prosper in Salford in 1880. Hobson's daughters — the first characters we see on stage — are dressed in black. This is possibly because they are in mourning; their mother, we learn later, is dead, and the Victorians often used to wear mourning for long periods of time by our standards. But black clothes are also economical because they do not show the dirt and need not be replaced very often. We also notice that they are wearing aprons, which shows that they have to work for a living.

The two youngest of Hobson's daughters are in the shop when the curtain rises. The stage directions show that although they are at the counter they are not working: Alice is knitting and Vickey is reading. When Maggie enters, however, she occupies herself with the accounts book. Brighouse makes it clear, in this small but telling detail, that the sisters have different attitudes to work. Their immediate conversation is about their father, who has not been down for breakfast yet because he was at a Masons' meeting the night before. Since it is already noon, according to the stage directions, we may already be able to guess the reason for Hobson's late rising: he has had too much to drink.

Albert Prosser, Alice's suitor, is the first person to enter the shop from the street. He intends to have a word with Alice, thinking that Hobson will already be out. Albert and Alice address each other formally as 'Mr' and 'Miss' as well-bred people might be expected to do in 1880. But as soon as he is told that Hobson is still in, Albert tries to leave. He is stopped by Maggie, who obviously does not feel that people should just drop into the shop to pass the time of day. She uses the fact that Albert feels slightly guilty to force him into buying a new pair of boots. To begin with, Albert agrees to buy something — a pair of shoelaces, because they are the cheapest thing he can think of. Perhaps Albert at first thinks that Maggie is playing a practical joke; but the stage directions say that when Albert simpers at her, she does not smile in response. He is completely outmanoeuvred by Maggie who is trying to make a point both to him and to Alice, who is watching. She then shows Albert out, Alice protests, and Maggie makes it clear that her intention was to discourage him from coming in. Alice's retort is spiteful — 'It's all very well for an old maid like you to talk' — but, as she adds, their father will not let them go out to court.

Hobson himself now enters. Again, the stage directions give us clues to the sort of man he is: 'coarse' is not a complimentary description, and we might think that someone who wears a gold chain with Masonic emblems is trying too hard to be noticed. His first words confirm such suspicions. He tells his daughters that he is going out for a quarter of an hour; their ironic comments make it clear that they know he is actually going to the Moonraker's Inn. They want him to be back before his dinner is ruined. Hobson resents his daughters' refusal to take him at his word and their attempt to make sure that he will not be late home for dinner. He gives them a lecture on what he calls their uppishness and bumptiousness. He turns his attack to the new bustle dresses which Alice and Vickey have been seen wearing, and which seem to him immodest. He then pompously links the question of fashion with wider issues of decency, intelligence, and even the British Constitution. Although he declares that he stands 'for common-sense and sincerity', his arguments are exaggerated and illogical. Just as the girls are obviously used to their father going out to the Moonraker's for an hour or more at midday, they are also obviously used to Hobson's arguments, and do not intend to obey him in the matter of fashionable dress. Hobson's final answer to his daughters' 'uppishness' is to abandon argument altogether. He declares he will not solve the problem himself, but pass it onto others by marrying Alice and Vickey off to husbands of his choice.

The argument which began about bustles has ignored Maggie, who is not as interested in the new fashion as her sisters. But she asks her father whether he is going to find her a husband as well. Hobson is amazed at the question, and retorts unkindly that she is too old to marry, and that she is a real old maid.

Maggie says very little at this point. When she reminds Hobson that his dinner will be ready for one o'clock, he rejoins that he sets the hours in the house, and that he — not Maggie — will determine when one o'clock dinner is served. Maggie answers, 'Yes, father', although her tone could be one of mock-resignation or irony. What is clear is that Hobson always likes to have the last word, and that Maggie is thinking about something.

Having reasserted his authority, as he thinks, Hobson prepares to leave again. He is prevented from doing so by the arrival of Mrs Hepworth in her carriage outside the shop. She is a wealthy customer with whom Hobson feels he must deal personally. His attitude changes immediately to one of servile attentiveness. He overdoes the politeness, because when he fondles the boots she has come about she humiliates him by telling him to stop it. She wants to know who made the boots that Hobson sent her, and, because he assumes she has a complaint about them, Hobson is evasive. In exasperation Mrs Hepworth asks Maggie, and Maggie summons Tubby Wadlow from the workshop in the cellar. From Tubby they learn that the boots are Will Mossop's handiwork; and Will, too, is called up. Will is described as 'stunted mentally' but 'the raw material of a charming man'. He admits to making the boots, and Mrs Hepworth presents her visiting card with the words 'Take that'. Will cringes, expecting a blow. The effect of the command is comic, but it is also pitiful, and shows how downtrodden Will is at the beginning of the play. His backwardness is reinforced by his inability to read the card.

Hobson still misunderstands the situation, and promises that it will not occur again. But Mrs Hepworth tells him to be quiet and goes on to explain that the boots Will has made for her are the best she has ever bought. She insists that Will let her know if he should go to work anywhere else, and that in future he is to make boots for herself and her daughters. With a final comment that she expects Hobson does not pay Will what he is worth, she leaves.

Hobson's pride has been severely dented by his fawning in front of Mrs Hepworth and by her forthright and deflating comments. He resumes his blustering manner to compensate for his humiliation, declaring that he will never permit her to enter his shop again. But he is forced to change his attitude almost immediately, because at this point his friend Jim Heeler enters and expresses his surprise at seeing Mrs Hepworth's carriage outside Hobson's shop. Since it enhances his status with Jim to make the most of this connection, he lies again, pretending that she is a very old customer.

Hobson is worried about his daughters and, rather than discuss them in the Moonraker's, he sends them out of the shop and discusses them with Jim. Jim does not have the same problems as Hobson with his own daughters because his wife is still alive and will beat them if they do not behave. But Hobson, who was glad of the peace when his wife died, sees that he was wrong to feel relieved, since now there are three women dominating him instead of one. He complains that his daughters do not respect what he has to say, and when Jim tries to boost his self-esteem by likening him to John Bright, he sees through the flattery and refuses to be so easily consoled. Jim offers him more believable compliments—and Hobson accepts them!

Jim counsels against shouting, and suggests what Hobson had already proposed: marrying his daughters off. It is easy to see why these two men, with their identical patronising attitudes to women, are friends. Hobson is fussy about the husbands he will pick—he would like them to be non-drinkers, which is rather ironical in the light of what we already know about his drinking habits. Then Jim mentions that Hobson would not only have to pay for the weddings; he would also have to provide dowries, or 'settlements'. Hobson has not thought of this before, and he swiftly changes his plans, unwilling to purchase his peace at such a high price. During this exchange he confirms that he does not pay his daughters any wages. After a further brief altercation with Maggie about the time for dinner, he and Jim leave for the Moonraker's.

Maggie is now alone onstage. She calls Will Mossop up into the shop, and he enters unwillingly. He also hesitates when Maggie asks him to show her his hands. This could be because Will is shy, or because he has an idea of Maggie's plans for him, or both. Like Mrs Hepworth, Maggie praises Will's skill, and she goes on, trying to awaken his sense of ambition. But Will misunderstands what she is driving at, even thinking that his job might be at risk. Maggie tries to give him a sense of his own value by pointing out that it is his craftsmanship and her sales technique which keep the shop going. Will tries to escape back to his workshop now, but Maggie won't let him. Her next words, which seem to suggest a purely business partnership, allay his fears that she is proposing marriage. When he explains that he thought she was proposing marriage to him, she simply answers, 'I am.' This astounds him even more — she is the master's daughter!

Will is very honest. He admits that he is not in love with Maggie, neither is he ambitious. In addition, he is already engaged to Ada Figgins, the daughter of his landlady. He is also probably worried that Hobson might sack him. At this interchange, Will refers to Maggie as 'Maggie' rather than as 'Miss Maggie' as he did a few seconds before. This indicates that, whatever he says, his relationship with her has already become slightly more intimate. In this comic interchange, Will is still trying to reason Maggie out of her proposal. He wants her to leave him alone, but she replies, 'So does the fly when the spider catches him. You're my man, Will Mossop.' To her Will's lack of affection does not matter since she loves him, and Ada Figgins is a 'scheming hussy' who is clinging to him. She must be got rid of.

At this dramatically opportune moment, Ada enters with Will's lunch. Immediately, Maggie confronts her: 'You're treading on my foot, young woman,' she says. The scene is the reverse of that usually found in a romantic comedy in which two young men argue over one woman. Ada strongly opposes Maggie at first, but she loses the argument over who has the best plans for Will's future because she is relying completely on Will. Most comic of all is Will's plaintive protest that Ada is not fighting hard enough for him. When Ada can no longer argue herself, she threatens Will with her mother's wrath and leaves.

Will is afraid of Mrs Figgins, and we have already learned that she had a hand in his engagement to her daughter. Maggie simply organises things so that Will does not have to go back to his lodgings again by moving him in with Tubby. Will is full of admiration for the way she has arranged matters, and is aware of the advantages of a partnership with her. To round things off, Maggie asks Will to kiss her. Will knows that this would be a symbolic acceptance of everything Maggie has said so far and, as he hesitates, Alice and Vickey enter the shop. He swiftly bolts off into the cellar.

The two girls are amazed when Maggie casually announces that she is going to marry Will. They reveal themselves to be snobbish, refusing to accept Will as a brother-in-law. Alice fears also that the match will spoil her chances of marrying Albert Prosser. Hobson comes in, and after some more argument to prove he is head of the household, Maggie gives him the news. His first reaction is anger that his authority has been challenged; he thinks he is the only one entitled to choose husbands. Then he puts to Maggie the argument used by Alice: that Will is her social inferior whose father was illegitimate. He is more worried about his neighbourhood image than about Maggie's future happiness.

Maggie tells her father her terms—that now she is getting married she will want to be paid wages. The mention of money touches Hobson on his sore spot, and he reacts by taking off his belt and calling Will up. Although Will insists—correctly—that he hasn't 'taken up' with Maggie, Hobson prepares to strike. Will warns him that if he is hit, he will take Maggie 'and stick to her like glue'. Hobson's pride forces him to deliver the blow, and Will makes good his threat. He kisses her—which he would not do before —and promises that if Hobson beats him again he will leave the shop with Maggie for good. Maggie, overjoyed at Will's new strength of character, embraces him. Hobson is left standing in amazement.

NOTES AND GLOSSARY:

Masons:	short for 'Freemasons', a self-elected secret society, founded in the eighteenth century, usually made up of the most wealthy and powerful members of the community
make sheep's eyes:	gaze adoringly; ogle
florid:	of red complexion, sometimes caused by drinking too much alcohol
uppishness:	arrogance
bumptious:	over-confident, pushy
guys:	dummies dressed strangely, like Guy Fawkes
publican:	landlord of a public house
hump added to nature:	a bustle, a framework worn under a dress at the back, just below waist-level, and intended to make a long skirt hang gracefully
old maid:	a woman past marriageable age
leathering:	beating, hitting with a belt
fell on rest:	a euphemism for 'died'
John Bright:	(1811–89) a great nineteenth-century orator and parliamentarian. He was particularly honoured in Lancashire as a leading member of the Anti-Corn Law League and as a champion of Free Trade
gift of the gab:	eloquence
moithered:	beset with problems
temperance:	those who were members of Temperance Societies, pledged never to touch alcohol

settlements:	dowries
owt:	anything
feared:	afraid
dost:	short for 'dost thou', meaning 'do you'
axing:	asking
by gum:	an alternative to the blasphemous 'By God!'
near the bone:	very basic, without luxuries or comforts
body:	person
tokened:	engaged
jaw:	talk at someone
the banns:	an announcement of a forthcoming marriage which is read out in church for three Sundays before the wedding
finicking:	fussy
nowt:	nothing
come-by-chance:	illegitimate child
brass:	money
gradely:	large amount

Act II

The second act is set in Hobson's shop again, one month later. This means that the three weeks necessary for the banns to be read have passed, and it is time for the wedding of Maggie and Will.

It is clear from the beginning that Vickey and Alice have no idea of how to run the shop in Maggie's absence. They can neither cope with the accounts nor give orders to Tubby when he asks for them. He comments on the marked decline of the high-class trade during the past month, and adds that clogs alone will not even pay the rent, quite apart from the wages. As he descends into the cellar, Tubby mentions that Maggie has left, and from this we can guess that she must have left with Will. As Tubby, Alice and Vickey haggle over whether he is being given an order or not, it becomes clear that nobody in the shop is prepared to take responsibility for giving orders. Tubby leaves, and Alice and Vickey now argue with each other. During the course of this exchange, we learn that Hobson is now spending more time than ever in the Moonraker's. When Alice says she wishes she was safely married and away from home, Vickey agrees with her, revealing that she also has a suitor. But neither of the girls thinks they will be married because nobody will be keen to have Will Mossop for a brother-in-law. It is clear that the girls blame Maggie for the situation in which they find themselves.

Maggie now enters, followed by Freddy Beenstock (Vickey's suitor) and Will. Freddy is dressed more smartly than the other two, although Maggie and Will are about to be married. Although Alice is surprised by Maggie's entrance, it does not stop either her or Vickey blaming Maggie and Will for their woes. In particular, Hobson has become very difficult about his daughters seeing their young men, and Albert has not been round so often since Maggie sold him a pair of boots. But Maggie tells them that she has come to help them, and she sends Freddy off to fetch Albert Prosser and a 'paper'. What the paper deals with we are not told. Before Freddy leaves, however, he reveals that Hobson, returning home drunk, has fallen into a cellar in his corn warehouse through a trapdoor in the pavement. He is not hurt, but is sleeping soundly.

With Freddy gone, the snobbishness of Vickey and Alice displays itself again. After Vickey has pointed out that Hobson changed his mind about their marriages because of the marriage of Maggie and Will, Alice remarks on Will's low social standing. Maggie deals with their complaints by telling them that she will arrange their marriages, but that they must change their attitude to Will. She insists that they both kiss him as a token of their acceptance of him into the family, saying that Will is now as good as they are because he is his own master — he has established his own premises and had his own cards printed. Taken aback by Will's sudden rise in the world the girls kiss him, although under protest. Will is surprised to find that kissing young women is much more pleasant than he expected. It is a sign that his shyness is not as bad as it was, but Maggie tells him firmly, 'Don't get too fond of it, my lad.'

Only at this point are the girls told that it is Maggie's and Will's wedding-day, and that they are invited to the wedding with Albert and Freddy. Maggie seems to know that the high-class trade has been leaving Hobson's recently, and she tells her sisters that because trade is slack they can let Tubby look after the shop while they are out. When they protest she points out that they have already approved by kissing the bridegroom. They are even more astonished when Maggie tries on a brass ring for size to use as a wedding ring, and insists on paying fourpence for it. 'A ring out of stock!' exclaims Alice. Maggie's down-to-earth rejoinder is 'They're always out of someone's stock.'

Ensuing discussion about what is necessary to furnish a home gives Maggie the cue to order Will to remove some broken-down chairs and a sofa from the lumber-room upstairs. She tells her sisters that Will can mend the chairs in time for the wedding-feast at their new home. The fact that their home is to be two cellars also appals Alice and Vickey. When they wonder whether the chairs Will is taking might be of some use to themselves, Maggie silences them by explaining that she has a plan to get them marriage-settlements.

She refuses to say any more about her plan at this point, and sends her sisters out to put on their hats for the wedding, just as Freddy and Albert enter. She enlists Freddy to help Will with moving the furniture, and reads from a legal document Albert has drawn up according to her instructions. It is an action against Hobson for trespass and damages committed on the Beenstock premises. Albert is not sure whether the document is good law or not, but Maggie tells him that the case will not come to court, and directs Freddy to take the paper and place it on *her* father in *his* cellar.

It is now almost time for the wedding. The furniture has been loaded onto a hand-cart outside and, since everyone else is either busy or about to set off for the wedding, Albert is told to take it round to Maggie's and Will's new home. He is afraid that he might be seen by people he knows, and ridiculed, but he knows that there is no choice if he wants Maggie to carry out her plan. Because business is so slack, Maggie is able to put Tubby in charge of the shop.

Everything is now set for the wedding. But before they leave for church, Maggie asks Will how he feels about it. He tells her that his mind is made up, although he does not sound too enthusiastic. When she asks him again whether he can be honest in saying 'yes', Will answers that he can: 'You're growing on me, lass.' Will's comment is truthful, and shows that although he does not yet love Maggie there is the prospect of future development in their relationship. How far they have to go, however, is emphasised when Alice and Vickey reappear in their best clothes, and Vickey asks Will whether he has the ring. It turns out that Maggie has it, because she does not trust Will to remember to bring it. As they all leave, Tubby throws old shoes after them — a traditional way of wishing good luck to a couple who are about to be married.

NOTES AND GLOSSARY:

play old Harry:	be enraged
nowty:	uncertain, unpredictable
look-out:	concern, problem
at sixes and sevens:	disorganised
a blood:	a dandy
you don't shape:	you do nothing about it
as lief:	rather, willingly
Flat Iron Market:	a second-hand goods market in Salford
sticks:	furniture
against you:	ready for when you
hash:	mess
fast:	secure; here, 'fast asleep'
Howst:	how are you
summat:	something
Sithee:	look here!
Yon:	that
toe the line:	behave oneself

Act III

Act III is set in Oldfield Road where Maggie and Will have their workshop and living-quarters. The cellar is cramped and sparsely furnished, as the stage directions make clear. In reverse lettering on the windows, visible to the audience, Will's name and trade can be seen—a sign of the couple's independence. They have been married, returned home with Vickey, Alice, Freddy and Albert, and finished the wedding-feast. Like the furniture, this is sparse: pork-pie and wedding-cake to eat, with only tea to drink. As the curtain rises the visitors are toasting the newly-weds.

Will responds to the toast in the traditional manner by making a short speech, which he has learned by heart. Although he stumbles over some words, and has to be prompted by Maggie at one point, in delivering his speech he shows a new self-confidence. After he has finished, Albert tries to give a speech in reply, but Alice tells him he has already had his turn. Freddy congratulates Will on his speech, and Vickey asks who taught it him. Although Will does not say, Alice guesses that it was Maggie and makes a jibe about it. Maggie admits that this is the case; she is educating Will, and she adds that in twenty years' time it will be Will whom the Bank will regard most highly of the three men.

Albert, Alice and Vickey want to know where Maggie and Will managed to find the money to set up the business. All that Maggie will say is that they had help from an outside source. She adds that the same source provided the hot-house flowers in the basin on the table, but although Albert exclaims 'Ah!' in a knowing sort of way, the identity of the mystery benefactor is not disclosed.

By now the girls are wondering whether they should be at home, since Hobson may by now be back there in a bad temper. As they prepare to leave with Albert and Freddy, Maggie asks Will to clear the table. Freddy and Albert are incredulous that Will agrees to this; they obviously regard such chores as 'women's work', beneath the dignity of men. Maggie responds by ordering them to help Will with the clearing and washing-up.

At this point there is a knock at the door upstairs. Maggie has hung a sign up saying 'Business suspended for the day' and is prepared to let whoever it is carry on knocking, until Hobson's voice is heard. Everyone except Maggie is worried; according to the stage directions, Vickey is terrified. While they are panicking, Maggie ushers them all, apart from Will, into the bedroom. She wants Will to stay because he must show that he is the 'gaffer', or head of the household.

Maggie answers the door to Hobson, but before she lets him in she insists that she must have Will's permission. After he has been allowed in, Hobson has to make things up with Will by shaking hands with him. Even at this stage, Will is so apprehensive at the thought of being left alone with Maggie that he expresses his hope that Hobson will be able to stay a long time. Maggie is more businesslike, asking her father to sit down for a moment, pouring him a cup of tea, and insisting that he eats a slice of wedding-cake as a token of his acceptance of the marriage. At length he complies with her request, although he hates sweet food.

The most noticeable thing about Hobson in this act is how subdued he is by comparison with his earlier appearances. This is due to a combination of drink, which has given him a headache, and anxiety about the legal document with which he has been served. He is less blustering and less sure of himself, and he desperately needs Maggie's advice. She, however, will not hear of such a thing and tells Hobson to discuss his problems with Will in a man-to-man way, with no woman present. She is trying to force him to acknowledge that his dismissive comments about women were false and unjustified. Even if he must speak to her, she argues, it must be with Will present because he is now 'family'. She also tells Will that he must call Hobson 'Father' from now on — something which astonishes Will as much as it does Hobson himself. But Hobson eventually starts discussing his problem with Will still present.

Hobson explains that he is ruined, producing the legal document which He calls 'a stab in the back', taking a mean, cowardly advantage of an accident. Typically, Hobson blames the entire incident on someone else — Maggie, who has driven him to over-indulge at the Moonraker's by her thankless behaviour. His terror of lawyers emerges in his self-pitying rantings but, far from comforting him, Maggie encourages him to believe that the worst might happen. She does, however, establish that Hobson only trespassed accidentally.

What Hobson is most worried about is the case coming to court. If it does, he will not only lose the esteem of his neighbours but also custom, since his better customers will stop patronising a man who has had to admit publicly in a court of law that he was drunk at twelve o'clock in the morning. Maggie intentionally, and Will unintentionally, encourage Hobson to believe that his name will appear in the newspapers. Hobson's fear is partly the product of his own vanity: he believes he will make news because he regards himself as a man of importance. Will unwittingly provokes Hobson into losing his temper, but Maggie knows that the more worried by disgrace Hobson is, the more easily he will fall in with her plans. She cleverly leads the discussion towards the idea of an out of court settlement. Hobson thinks this is a good suggestion, but would rather not enter a lawyer's office where he thinks he would be pressed for money twice as hard as he would be in court. This provides Maggie with the perfect cue to call Albert and the others out of the bedroom.

Hobson's first reaction to the appearance of his daughters is anger that the shop has been left with only Tubby to look after it. He is obviously not completely cowed by his experience, and when Albert suggests that they get down to business, Hobson interrupts him with the retort 'Honest men live by business and lawyers live by the law.' He has already reiterated his warning that there will not be another wedding in the family for a long time, but no sooner has he said this than he unknowingly provides the money for his daughters' dowries.

Albert at first suggests a thousand pounds to settle out of court. Even Maggie, however, thinks this is too high. She warns Albert and Freddy that if they are too greedy there will be a counter-action against Beenstock's for negligence in leaving the trapdoor open. This also gives Hobson the impression that Maggie is trying to beat the figure down as low as possible, and makes him more amenable to her suggestion that he pay five hundred pounds. He still only agrees to it after a further reminder from her that the alternative is being exposed in court. But once he has agreed to it, as Albert points out, his word is as good as his bond. It is now safe to reveal the trick which has been played on Hobson in order to force him to part with money for his daughters' marriage settlements.

When he learns the truth, Hobson is outraged, and blames Maggie for organising things as he picks up his hat and storms out. Before leaving he warns the prospective husbands that they will find married life a costly business.

Once Hobson has left, it is the turn of the other four visitors to leave. As they do so, they invite Maggie and Will to their own weddings. Will would still like them to stay, but they all leave, and Maggie clears the table for Will's lesson while he fetches his slate. The old exercise reads 'There is always room at the top'. After cleaning the slate she sets Will the similarly encouraging motto 'Great things grow from small' to copy.

Maggie reveals the warmer side of her nature by keeping one of the hot-house flowers to press in her Bible as a souvenir of the wedding, at the same time revealing to the audience that their benefactor was Mrs Hepworth. The act ends without words. Will stays to finish his writing after Maggie has gone to bed. When he has finished, he takes off his boots and collar and moves towards the bedroom door. But shyness overcomes him and, after more vacillation, he puts out the light and lies down to sleep on the sofa. Soon afterwards Maggie reappears in her nightdress and leads him by the ear to the bedroom. The action is both comic and moving, and perfectly exemplifies Maggie's practical but tender nature.

NOTES AND GLOSSARY:

tackle:	tools and working materials
wrong road:	wrong way
wind-up:	conclusion
stewed:	brewed for too long
Happen:	perhaps
Manchester Guardian:	founded as a daily newspaper in Manchester in 1855, under the editorship of C.P. Scott (1846–1932), it became the voice of Liberalism. Brighouse wrote for it, but since 1959 'Manchester' has been dropped from its title and it has become a London newspaper

chances:	happens
jumped-up:	unworthily risen in the world, presumptuous
cock-a-hooping:	triumphant
mused:	bemused
libellous:	in law, destroying good character by the spoken word
diddled:	cheated
keep:	maintenance costs

Act IV

Act IV takes place in Hobson's living-room, which is next to the shop of Acts I and II. The room is cluttered and dirty because Alice and Vickey have now also left Hobson and he, we may guess, has continued his downward slide. The time is one morning, a year after Act III, and the curtain rises on Tubby Wadlow ineptly trying to lay the table and cook Hobson's breakfast at the same time. Before any words are spoken we have been made aware of the worsening of Hobson's domestic circumstances.

Jim Heeler appears. He has been sent for by Hobson, who says he is very ill. But Tubby tells Jim that Hobson will soon be coming down for breakfast. He also tells him that Dr MacFarlane has been sent for. Nothing more is said about the nature of Hobson's illness, although the fact that he has sent for a friend as well as a doctor provides the audience with a clue.

While they are waiting for Hobson, Jim and Tubby discuss the problems from which his business is suffering. Tubby complains that housework is not for him, although he has to agree with Jim that he does not have his time taken up much with making boots and clogs these days. Jim is not sure that Tubby ought to be talking so frankly about his master's affairs with him. But Tubby is keen to talk, and claims he has as much right to as anyone else. Furthermore, he blames Hobson's pride, his temper and his obstinacy — rather than competition from Maggie and Will — for the decline of the business, as well as the fact that Hobson is employing male assistants in the shop.

When Hobson enters, his speech is full of melancholy and self-pity. Jim Heeler suggests that what his friend needs is a woman about the house. Tubby volunteers to go to fetch Maggie. It is obvious that Hobson is in a bad way, not just from the fact that he is unshaven and collarless but also because he does not dispute this suggestion. He does not seem to care much whether Tubby fetches Maggie or not. He complains about his daughters' desertion, saying that when he is dead of neglect they will be sorry for their behaviour. He explains that he has not washed or shaved; the water made him wish to drown himself, and he was afraid he would cut his throat with the razor.

Finally, after bewailing his fate, Hobson admits that the cause of his illness is alcohol. As Jim disputes this with him, Dr MacFarlane enters.

The stage directions describe the doctor simply as 'domineering'. He behaves in accordance with this description straight away since he has been falsely told that his patient was too ill to get out of bed, and so has come at once in spite of having been up most of the night attending a childbirth. Both Hobson and Jim are taken aback by the doctor's bluntness. He tells them that they both have their fate written on their faces—meaning that they are both alcoholics. He goes on to link Hobson's physical complaints to his psychological condition: 'Your complaint and your character are the same,' he says. Finally he refuses to make his diagnosis until Jim leaves him alone with his patient. Hobson eventually persuades Jim to leave; but only, he says, so that he can teach the doctor a lesson. Jim then leaves.

Hobson candidly describes his symptoms to the doctor, who diagnoses chronic alcoholism. But when he writes out a prescription, Hobson says that he will not take it, to which the doctor's answer is that Hobson has drunk himself almost to death and would be insane not to follow medical advice. When the doctor also adds that Hobson must practise total abstinence, he refuses. He changes the view he expressed to Jim, asserting that his drinking is no more than 'reasonable refreshment'. Simply in order to oppose what the doctor wants he is prepared to go down to the Moonraker's immediately.

Although Hobson offers Dr MacFarlane his fee, the doctor refuses to take it. He is at least as stubborn as Hobson, who has now made him very angry. His anger shows itself in his Scottish accent, which becomes thicker as he shouts down Hobson's bravado. He finds out that the most 'uppish' of Hobson's daughters is Maggie and, knowing that his patient must have firm discipline from someone, he prescribes her as well. Hobson will not hear of this, but the doctor insists, having taken a liking to his patient and being determined to save him.

Just as the doctor is saying her name, Maggie walks in. Tubby has obviously been to her. When Hobson hears this he threatens to sack Tubby; he is embarrassed that anyone else might find out about his drink problem. When Dr MacFarlane tells her bluntly that her father is drinking himself to death, Maggie asks for more details. Hobson calls this 'Just nasty-minded curiosity', but Maggie has a right to know more before she makes a decision on whether or not to sacrifice her own home. Looking after Hobson will mean moving into his house and running the household.

The doctor does not leave with his tail between his legs, as Hobson imagines, but confident that Maggie will be able to deal with her father. But nothing is definite yet. The first thing Maggie does is to send Tubby off to get the prescription made up and fetch Will. She then tells Hobson that he can be cured, but that she cannot make the decision to leave the business on Oldfield Road to look after him without Will's consent. Hobson mocks her, saying that asking Will is merely a matter of form because he is not the master of his house. By this stage it is clear that Hobson does want one of his daughters back to look after him, and that he would prefer it to be Maggie. He believes that he has more call on Maggie's attention than her husband and also that it is her duty as the eldest daughter to come back and nurse him.

At this point Alice enters. Brighouse tells us that she looks rather elaborately dressed for so early in the day, and that she appears 'languidly haughty' — a description confirmed by her first words to Maggie. When Maggie, in reply to Alice's question, tells her that she has been with her father for some time, Alice's snobbish response is that a solicitor's wife does not get up as early as a cobbler's wife. But Maggie ignores this attempt to lord it over her, and tells her that their father is ill and that one of them must look after him. Alice, however, is not prepared to sacrifice her new home in the Crescent. Her indifference to his plight shocks Hobson, but she agrees with him in thinking that it is Maggie's duty to return.

Vickey enters next. She is gushingly emotional towards Hobson, having heard that he is ill. His reaction is just as effusive, but as soon as Vickey realises what is required she releases herself from Hobson's grasp and says that she cannot be expected to look after him as she is pregnant.

Maggie's response is to change the subject by asking her father to put on a collar before Will comes. The others ridicule her suggestion; they have a snobbish attitude towards Will and think that Maggie is only pretending to be concerned about Will's dignity. After Maggie theatens to go if he does not, Hobson agrees, but insists that he is not complying out of respect for Will, but because his neck is cold.

While Hobson leaves to put on his collar, the three sisters take the opportunity to discuss which of them is to return and look after him. Both Vickey and Alice are very unwilling and make excuses. Alice claims it is Maggie's duty, and Vickey spitefully adds that living in her father's house should be a pleasure to Maggie after living in cellars. But Maggie tells them she has had to put up with Hobson for thirty years already and, in any case, she must consult Will first. Vickey insults Will again, saying that he lacks spirit. Maggie calmly replies that Will has perhaps changed since Vickey last met him. The restraint of her comment prepares us for the appearance of Will, whom Maggie now hears moving about in the shop, and for any change in his character.

While Maggie goes off to the shop to talk to Will about what the doctor has said, Alice and Vickey have second thoughts about letting her and Will move in to look after their father. They are afraid that Hobson might reward Maggie's and Will's care by making them the main beneficiaries of his will. In order to prevent this, Alice suggests that they get Albert to draw up Hobson's will for him as soon as possible. They also worried that Maggie is coaching Will on what to say, so Vickey opens the shop door to see what is happening. She is amazed to find Will up on a ladder inspecting Hobson's stock, and even more amazed when in reply to her objections he tells her that he wants to know what he is coming into before committing himself. Alice is so surprised that she exclaims 'That's never Willie Mossop'. These reactions, like Maggie's comment earlier, prepare us for the change made explicit in the stage directions which follow. As Will enters, he is described as looking prosperous and self-confident.

We immediately see how much Will has changed, because almost the first thing he does is order Maggie about! He tells her to go and fetch her father because he is wasting time when he could be working. He goes on to tell the girls that Hobson's business is worth no more than two hundred pounds—a figure which shocks them, perhaps because of their earlier conversation about the will. To make his point, Will tells Vickey that she ought to know the true value of a business because her husband is in trade. The remark infuriates Vickey, who obviously likes to pretend that there is a difference in social standing between the wholesale business of Beenstock's and 'trade'—the retail business of Will and Maggie.

Both Alice and Vickey still speak to Will as if he is their hired boot-hand to whom the value of Hobson's ought to be of no concern. Alice tries to put Will in his place by declaring that he will do what he is told. But Will makes it clear that he and Maggie will only move in with Hobson on their own terms. The squabbling continues, with Will making the last point when he reminds the girls of the help he and Maggie gave them in arranging their marriage-portions.

Maggie and Hobson enter, and Will is polite to his father-in-law to begin with. But when Will says he does not want to waste time, Hobson asks whether his shop is more important than his father-in-law's life. Will refuses to be distracted by this, saying Hobson's welfare only worries him because it worries Maggie. Even Maggie is slightly taken aback by Will's sharp tone, and Will almost gives himself away when he lets drop that she told him to take a high hand. But when Will then tells the protesting girls that there is no need for them to stay, Hobson temporarily supports him. He points out that neither of them is prepared to look after him. When they answer that they want to protect him against Will, Hobson loses his temper at the mere idea. He evidently still has the same low opinion of Will that he had a year before.

Hobson forces Alice and Vickey to say that they will not come back to look after him, confident that Maggie will do so. He thinks he is in control of the situation, despite his weakness, and when Alice and Vickey refuse to help he orders them out of the house. Will opens the door for them, and Maggie tries to soften her father's harshness by inviting her sisters to come to tea some time. But they are too bitter to leave with anything but insults. 'Beggars on horseback,' Vickey comments as she leaves, which is ironic: the phrase describes her own attitude rather than that of Maggie and Will.

As soon as the girls have left, Hobson makes what he considers to be a generous proposal to Maggie and Will. If they come back to live with him, he says, Will can have his old job back on his old wages while Maggie looks after himself, the house, and the shop. He tells them that he regards his offer as handsome, giving them rent-free accommodation, and paying for half of housekeeping expenses. Despite being very ill only a few minutes before, Hobson is now more his old self. He is prepared to bargain because the terms he has spelt out are obviously unacceptable to Maggie and Will. Even if Hobson is bargaining at this point, however, he is taken aback by Will's and Maggie's reaction. In fact, the stage directions say he is 'incredulous' — he seems not to be able to believe that they could turn down such a good offer. For Maggie and Will, Hobson's proposals are ridiculous. They are wasting their time and they rise to leave.

Will now tells Hobson the truth of his situation, making his longest speech in the play. He explains that he and Maggie have worked hard and prospered; they have paid off their loan from Mrs Hepworth and taken Hobson's high-class trade away from him. Hobson's business is now reduced to selling clogs, but all he can offer them is the old wages and jobs as though nothing has changed. Hobson is still living in the past, as his reaction to Will's speech proves: 'But—but—you're Will Mossop, you're my old shoe-hand.'

Hobson's interruption spurs Will on to stating his own terms for moving back. He tells Hobson that he will transfer to Hobson's premises, taking his father-in-law into partnership on condition that he stays as a 'sleeping partner' — that is, one who does not interfere with the way the business is run. While Hobson is rendered almost speechless, Will confidently moves on to the question of what the new business is to be called, as though the matter is already settled.

Will's proposal to name the business 'William Mossop, late Hobson' brings a protest from Maggie. The two of them spend a few seconds arguing over the name. Hobson remains silent and in the background. Will and Maggie are acting as though he has already agreed to everything else. The result is a compromise and they settle on 'Mossop and Hobson' as a name.

By now Will is in his element and he starts proposing more practical alterations to Hobson's premises: new chairs and carpets in order to 'pamper' the customers. He is so overbearing with Hobson now that when Hobson exclaims 'Alterations in my shop!' Will dismissively answers, 'In mine', before continuing. When Hobson asks whether Will thinks he is in St Anne's Square, Manchester, a high-class shopping area, Will answers that a move there is only a matter of time. He concludes by suggesting that Maggie take her father down to Albert Prosser's to get a legal deed of partnership drawn up.

Throughout this act the audience will have enjoyed seeing Will turn the tables first on Maggie's snobbish sisters and then on Hobson. When he makes his final suggestion and Hobson simply says 'I'll go and get my hat', we know he has completely reversed the position he was in at the beginning of the play. According to the stage directions, Hobson is pathetic and obedient at this point—it is the 'Hobson's Choice' of the title. In his absence Maggie and Will have the last scene of the play together. Will is almost sorry for Hobson, feeling that he has treated him too harshly. It is obvious that Will's words to Hobson were an expression of his own self-confidence, as well as being part of a plan he had discussed before with Maggie. He is still surprised by his new power and he admits to Maggie that he was not as confident as he sounded. In particular he confesses he was worried when it came to arguing with Maggie over the name for the business. She tells him not to spoil things by giving her too much of the credit for the victory over Hobson. 'You're the man I've made you and I'm proud,' she says, meaning that he is now his own boss.

The play ends with Will trying to persuade Maggie to accept a gold ring which he has bought to replace the brass ring they were married with. Maggie says she will wear it, but only if she can keep the old one to remind her of their humble beginnings and stop her from becoming too proud. She touches Will with affection and he kisses her, and Hobson appears with his hat on ready to go to the lawyer's. The last words of the play are Will's expression of his 'amazement, triumph and incredulity': 'Well, by gum!'

NOTES AND GLOSSARY:

Antimacassars:	cloths laid on the back of chairs or sofas to protect them from men's hair-oil
cut line:	product in which there is little profit
knockout:	overpowering person
ken:	(*Scottish*) know
sagacity:	wisdom
hanky-panky:	messing about, foolishness
pay . . . on the nail:	pay an agreed price for something directly, in cash
hae na:	have not
ma mannie:	my man
dunderheaded:	stupid
thraldom:	enslavement, magic spell
crack:	chat, discussion
I doubt:	I suspect
so what:	whatever
shut of:	free of
worrits:	worries
jibbing at:	unwilling to do something
cretonne:	unglazed, colour-printed cotton cloth
morocco:	type of soft leather for furnishings

Part 3

Commentary

English theatre in the early twentieth century

For the greater part of the nineteenth century the English stage was dominated by a variety of melodramas, extravaganzas and attempts to revive poetic drama. It was not until the 1890s that contemporary plays of lasting value began to appear with the work of Sir Arthur Pinero (1855–1934), H.A. Jones (1851–1929), Oscar Wilde (1854–1900) and George Bernard Shaw (1856–1950). By the turn of the century it was possible to speak of a rebirth of English drama.

One of the strongest forces for change in the theatre had come from Europe where, since the 1880s, a new naturalism had been showing itself in the work of playwrights such as the Swedish writer August Strindberg (1849–1912), the Russian Anton Chekhov (1860–1904), and the great Norwegian dramatist Henrik Ibsen (1828–1906). Ibsen's plays, employing naturalistic speech and dealing with the problems of contemporary society, were a profound influence on the leading English-language dramatist of the first quarter of the twentieth century, Shaw. Like Ibsen, Shaw intended his plays to be a challenge to conventional social attitudes on subjects such as sexual morality, class or religion, as well as being entertainments. Other playwrights, including John Galsworthy (1867–1933) and Harley Granville-Barker, also wrote plays that set out to deal with important social issues.

These developments also encouraged a number of regional playwrights who appeared in the years before the First World War. Aided by the growing Repertory Movement which helped to counter the London bias of British theatre, regional playwrights were able to have plays dealing with local subjects and written in local dialects produced in the major provincial cities. Harold Brighouse was very much a typical product of these developments, a playwright who dealt with characters in a recognisably Lancashire setting.

The Repertory Movement

Despite the lively, experimental approach of the new playwrights, it was at first impossible to stage serious new drama outside London. This was because the stage was virtually dominated by actor-managers with their own touring companies. These were based in the capital and only toured the provinces with guaranteed commercial successes. The system encouraged an appeal to the lowest common denominator, and by the end of the nineteenth century most theatres outside London had no companies attached to them; they simply existed to be hired by London impresarios.

The difficulty of staging new drama in theatres whose managers had no interest in it applied even to London, and it prompted Harley Granville-Barker and J.E. Vedrenne to launch an historic series of productions at the Court Theatre, London, between 1904 and 1907. Brighouse attended these seasons of new plays as a first-nighter when he worked in London, and they had a great effect on his own idea of what constituted good drama. Granville-Barker and Vedrenne established a nucleus of 'intellectual' plays as their basic repertory at the Court Theatre. Over half of the performances given at the Court were of plays by Shaw, but other major playwrights represented included Ibsen and Granville-Barker himself, as well as the classical Greek tragedians. The Court Theatre seasons were immensely successful and influential and proved the existence of an audience for intelligent contemporary drama. But the movement did not end with the closure of the Court in 1907. Instead, a nationwide Repertory Movement developed, decentralising and extending the achievements of Vedrenne and Granville-Barker. Within a few years, most major British cities had their own Repertory Theatres and acting companies.

The 'Manchester School' of dramatists

The Manchester Repertory company was based at the Gaiety Theatre. It was established by Miss Horniman, a remarkable, wealthy patron of drama with a reputation for aiding the cause of contemporary drama. She had funded the first production of Shaw's *Arms and the Man* in 1894 and largely paid for the Abbey Theatre in Dublin in 1904. Following the success of these ventures she funded the Gaiety, which opened in 1908. Although somewhat eccentric, Miss Horniman was single-minded in her determination to champion good new drama. In order to help launch the Gaiety she offered cash prizes to attract new scripts from local writers. To some extent these developments encouraged Brighouse to submit *Lonesome-like*, and his first play was produced at the Gaiety in 1909.

Miss Horniman's policy was to encourage dramatists who could deal with the experience of Lancashire people in their plays. This commitment was the common factor which linked the members of the 'Manchester School' of playwrights, of whom Brighouse, Stanley Houghton and Allan Monkhouse were the most successful. Brighouse and Houghton were particularly anxious to reflect Lancashire life in their plays. They used Lancashire speech, and Brighouse drew heavily on his own experience of the textile industry for subject-matter. Such a presentation of regional working life represented a further advance on the principles of the Repertory Movement, democratising its earlier appeal.

The themes of most of Brighouse's plays reflect the urban working- and lower-middle-class experience which had previously been denied dramatic expression. Although he was not an experimental playwright, Brighouse was something of an innovator in his use of city and industrial life as a subject. *The Price of Coal* and *Dealing in Futures*, two of his earliest plays, deal with industrial subjects, while the social drama makes itself felt in a play such as *Polygon*, which tackles the issue of housing. In *Garside's Career* Brighouse ventured into more directly political territory with a piece based on the mysterious disappearance of the Socialist M.P. Victor Grayson. Brighouse's plays, however, could never truly be called 'plays of ideas' in the sense of Shaw's plays. Nor was he a political radical. He did, however, believe that there was 'a touch of didacticism' in his better plays, which he declared were generally about 'the superficial somethings of a moderate optimist'.

Money, morality and class

The action of the play is generated by money and the need for financial security, and the morality of the characters in the play is mostly determined by the effect money has on them. One of the basic themes of *Hobson's Choice* is that of the progress from rags to riches through hard work. Apart from Mrs Hepworth, and Alice and Vickey in the final act, all of the characters have to work for a living. Throughout the play, Brighouse examines the different effects of the work ethic on these characters. He agrees with conventional morality by making those that work hard prosper, while those that do not, suffer or are viewed in a bad light. In this sense Brighouse is simply making his lower-middle-class characters adopt an appropriate set of middle-class values. The idea that hard work is necessary in order to get on in life is an idea which would have been familiar to an audience of 1916 from other literature, particularly the book *Self-Help* (1859) by Samuel Smiles (1812–1904), and would have been reinforced by a lifetime of church sermons as well as by school.

Hobson's Choice presents us with three main attitudes to money which roughly correspond to the main class divisions in society. At the bottom there are the working-class characters, Tubby Wadlow, Ada Figgins and Will Mossop. While they may work hard for their living, what they lack is ambition. Tubby, for example, is completely at a loss when Hobson's business starts to decline. At the beginning of Act II he has no idea what to do and will not even make clogs until he has managed to force Alice to give him an order to do so. This is despite the fact that he is the foreman and has been at Hobson's a long time. Ada is also without initiative or desire to 'better herself'. This is shown when Maggie asks her what her idea for the future is with Will, and she lamely answers that she trusts him to 'make the future right'.

At the beginning of the play Will is similarly resigned to his position in life. When Maggie tells him that if he marries Ada he will remain a boothand all his life, he simply replies that he is not ambitious. But under Maggie's influence, Will acquires the middle-class desire to become an independent businessman and do well for himself. Brighouse, however, is realistic enough to show that more than just hard work and ambition is necessary for success. Without Mrs Hepworth's loan Will and Maggie would never be able to set up their business. The same applies to the attempts by Alice and Vickey to escape their dependence on Hobson. They have to trick their father in order to marry and break free, like Maggie.

Mrs Hepworth, the only upper-class character in the play, is in a position where she can afford to ignore the need to make a living. Her complete independence means that she can speak her mind — it will not cost her anything if she offends someone. This attitude is shown clearly in her encounter with Hobson in Act I. Hobson is servile because he needs the quality trade which Mrs Hepworth represents; she, however, rebukes him for behaving in a ridiculous fashion. She is also very distant, referring to Maggie as 'young woman', Will as 'Mossop', and to Tubby simply as 'man'. This is because of the social gap between herself and the other characters. Nevertheless, she respects good workmanship, and has the money to pay for the best, whatever the cost.

Within the group of middle-class characters we find various different attitudes to work and money. We notice at the very beginning of the play that Alice and Vickey are reading and knitting in the shop while Maggie busies herself with an account book. Later, at the beginning of the second act, after Maggie and Will have left, the two younger sisters are unable to run the shop or give Tubby his orders. This attitude is reflected in their snobbishness towards those who do work, especially Will, whom they regard as lower than themselves. They also have a disdainful attitude towards Maggie because she is prepared to marry Will, to be married with a brass ring, to make use of second-hand furniture and to live in a cellar. These attitudes are based on differences in class. Vickey and Alice aspire to rise in society, not merely to be free of Hobson and his business. Their ambition is not to have to work at all. This is the reason for Alice's assumed superiority over Maggie in Act IV when she says that as a fashionable solicitor's wife she does not have to get up as early as a cobbler's wife. Brighouse intends this jibe to backfire on Alice, because he is writing for an audience which sees work as a positive virtue and thinks of 'fashionable solicitors' with some distrust.

Hobson's attitudes to money and work are contradictory. He has obviously worked hard in the past to build up his business; he is a self-made man who can boast: 'I'm a decent-minded man. I'm Hobson. I'm

British middle class and proud of it.' But he is now just resting on his laurels, letting other people do all the hard work for him. His claim to authority is therefore a hypocritical one, and his attitude is a parody of what a healthy work ethic should be. He rebukes Alice and Vickey for forgetting the middle-class virtues of hard work. But it is Hobson himself who has forgotten that money has to be earned. In this sense his alcoholism is a highly appropriate character flaw and a symbol of a disorientated set of values.

Maggie has the same down-to-earth attitude to the value of things that her father seems to have, but in her case it is genuine. She does not have any class-prejudice, but sometimes her view of the world can seem excessively based on money. For example, she refers to Will as 'a business idea in the shape of a man'; and we may think her comment at the wedding celebration that Will will be worth more at the Bank than the other two young men in twenty years' time rather crude. However, for all her practical money-consciousness, Maggie is the only member of her family who puts money into perspective. In her last speech to Will she makes clear her feeling that they should not forget their humble origins even if they become rich. Maggie's and Will's success is meant to show that it is necessary to work hard in order to prosper, but that it is possible to do it without becoming snobbish, hypocritical or hard-hearted.

Maggie and women's independence

In the late nineteenth century the question of political and social emancipation for women began to be debated. The character of the New Woman became a vital theme in literature of the time, and English dramatists were particularly influenced in their treatment of it by plays such as Ibsen's *A Doll's House* (first seen in England in 1881). Granville-Barker dealt with the subject in his *The Marrying of Ann Leete* (1899), as did Shaw in *Arms and the Man* (1894), *Man and Superman* (1901–3), *Major Barbara* (1905), and several other plays. The issue of women's rights is as alive in our own time as it was in the years around the turn of the century, and gives additional interest to Brighouse's use of the subject in *Hobson's Choice*.

The social background to the plays of Shaw, Granville-Barker and Brighouse was the Suffragette movement. Formed in 1903 as the W.S.P.U. (Women's Social and Political Union) the movement aimed to win the right to vote for women. In doing so it raised a whole host of related questions about women's rights in law, education and work and was regarded as a threat to society by governments of the day which steadfastly refused to consider granting women the rights they were demanding. Faced with a lack of progress in their campaign of moral persuasion, radical elements of the W.S.P.U. split away in 1912 to form a group which used more direct methods — burning letter-boxes, attacking government ministers, chaining themselves to the railings of Buckingham Palace and organising hunger strikes. The outbreak of the First World War put an end to these developments, and at the time *Hobson's Choice* was written the question of votes for women was still undecided.

The Suffragette movement was news at the time Brighouse's play appeared; its historical setting of thirty-five years before, however, resulted in making Maggie seem even more unusual in her determination to succeed. It has been said that Maggie does not quite have the independence of spirit of some of Shaw's heroines who choose not to marry, but the play makes it clear that Maggie must marry if she is to break free. Unlike the average Shavian heroine, she is not financially independent. In some ways her action is more courageous because she has more to lose.

Brighouse also makes quite clear the plight of women at the time the play is set. The way that Hobson expresses his belief that his daughters are property he can dispose of in the first act is an example of this. But Maggie flouts her father's wishes by marrying someone he disapproves of, and devising the plan which raises the money to enable her sisters to do the same. She also overturns convention in other ways. It is she, for example, who courts Will and organises their wedding, even down to the detail of carrying the ring to church—a task usually performed by the best man. When Freddy and Albert laugh at Will because he obeys when asked to clear the table, Maggie forces them to help him. It is clear that they object to helping not simply because they are guests, but because they regard clearing away pots and washing-up as women's work which is beneath them. Maggie's drive and energy and intelligence mean that, by the end of the play, all of the male characters have had to rely on her in one way or another. Even Dr MacFarlane concludes by 'prescribing' her for Hobson.

Even after marriage, Maggie is seen as an independent character, in contrast to her two sisters who regard themselves as their husbands' wives. Like Ada Figgins, Alice and Vickey rely on someone else to make all their important decisions for them. They present the usual response of women to social convention and, in doing so, make it possible for us to appreciate Maggie's achievement properly. Yet even Maggie herself eventually defers to tradition by marrying. She represents an attack on the restraints placed on women, but we should not forget that her motives are not idealistic. They are the result of her circumstances; Maggie has to use Will in order to escape the fate of becoming an embittered old woman working without wages for her father.

The play leaves us with the overall impression that women like Maggie are more than a match for men. Perhaps the most daring initiative of Maggie's for the audiences of 1916 was the last scene in Act III where she leads Will into the bedroom on their wedding night. This part of the play narrowly escaped the censor, because it challenged the Victorian belief that it was unthinkable and indecent to suggest that a respectable married woman could take the initiative in such a situation.

Love and marriage

In its anti-romantic attitude to love and marriage *Hobson's Choice* exploits the humorous potential of turning conventions upside down. This is most obvious in the scene when Maggie proposes to the reluctant Will, having relentlessly talked him into a corner. The situation of the woman pursuing the man deliberately reverses the procedure of traditional romantic comedy, as does the following confrontation between Maggie and Ada Figgins. Usually it is two men who fight over the single woman; here Brighouse creates humour with a theatrical paradox.

There are three marriages in the play, all of them based upon the importance of money. It seems at first that Will and Maggie are the couple most influenced by purely financial considerations. When Maggie's proposition is made, therefore, we are not surprised that it is straightforward and couched in the terms of a business arrangement. When Will asks her what she wants him for, she answers, 'To invest in. You're a business idea in the shape of a man.' This element is so strong that at first Will thinks Maggie is proposing nothing more than a business partnership, but his comic confusion is soon dispelled by Maggie. Even so, it is quite clear that this will be a marriage of convenience, at least to start with.

Alice's and Vickey's choices of husbands are also determined by the necessity for the girls to break away from their economic dependence on their father. Although they choose middle-class husbands—unlike Will, who is working class—they are in the same situation and act for the same motives as Maggie. Brighouse clearly shows that because the girls are marrying Freddy and Albert, they must take dowries with them. This was the traditional middle-class expectation of the time. Since Freddy and Albert will be keeping their wives they would expect dowries as a major contribution to the cost of setting up a joint household. Without dowries the girls would stand no chance of being married, no matter how eligible they might be in other ways.

Maggie turns tradition upside down on this point as well because she does not bring a dowry with her and has to carry on working after her marriage. To Alice and Vickey it is a sign of their superior status that their husbands can keep them without their having to work.

Alice and Vickey obviously believe in the conventional formalities of courtship before marriage. Maggie's exasperation with her sisters' attitude is demonstrated in the opening scene of the play when she prevents Albert from courting Alice in the shop. After she has shown Albert out she picks up a slipper to illustrate her opinion of romantic convention: to her a romantic courtship is a piece of useless glitter, like a fancy slipper.

However, the developing affection between Maggie and Will during the course of the play proves that although the marriage may have begun with all the love on one side—Maggie's—it is a partnership based on mutual regard by the end of Act IV.

Although at the end of Act III the audience is left with the impression that Maggie's and Will's marriage is going to be one in which Maggie dominates, they are disabused of the idea in Act IV where it becomes apparent that Maggie has made Will into her equal: 'You're the man I've made you and I'm proud,' she tells him. The respect that Maggie has insisted should be paid to Will as her husband has finally had the desired effect. On the other hand, Alice and Vickey dismiss their husbands as people whose views are unimportant. To them, husbands are merely providers of houses, furniture and babies.

Our last impression is that it is the least obviously 'romantic' of the three marriages, that between Maggie and Will, which contains the most genuine affection.

Hobson, drink and the temperance movement

Much of the action of *Hobson's Choice* stems from Hobson's growing addiction to alcohol. We are given hints about his excessive drinking at the beginning of the first act, hints which are confirmed by Hobson's dispute with his daughters soon after about his midday visit to the Moonraker's. Hobson's downward path grows steeper at the beginning of Act II when Vickey complains that he has been spending more time than ever at the Moonraker's since Maggie and Will left. How much Hobson's drinking has contributed to the obnoxious behaviour which drives Maggie and Will from the shop is a matter of interpretation; what is certain is that drink is responsible for Hobson falling through Beenstock's open trapdoor and into the snare of Maggie's plan to help Alice and Vickey. The chronic alcoholism diagnosed by Dr MacFarlane in Act IV is the logical outcome of a process which Brighouse shows developing from the very start of the play.

Alcohol plays a crucial role in *Hobson's Choice*. It was not by accident that Brighouse made this particular vice the flaw that brings Hobson low. Apart from furthering his plot and aptly symbolising Hobson's moral disorientation, drink allowed Brighouse to give the play more period authenticity. The 'Demon Drink' was a cliché of melodramatic Victorian literature, and Brighouse is perhaps trying to make his play more Victorian by using it. There is certainly some comic potential in the theme which Brighouse exploits; Hobson's evasions before his knowing daughters in Act I are funny, as is his self-pity, followed by defensive rantings, in Act IV. By setting his play in 1880, the heyday of the temperance movement, however, Brighouse was also drawing on historical details with which the majority of his audience would have been familiar.

The 1870s and 1880s were the decades of the highest consumption of alcohol recorded in British history. In part this was due to the wretched living conditions of the workers in the new industrial towns and cities; in a proverbial phrase, drink became 'the shortest way out of Manchester' for many people. It was in Manchester, too, that reaction against the tide of alcohol was sharpest. The largest temperance organisation in the country, the United Kingdom Alliance, was set up there in 1853. In its campaign to force governments to legislate on the availability of drink, the Alliance, along with other similar groups, most often found itself in support of the Liberal Party. Brighouse, like his father, was a Liberal supporter. Political sympathy as well as the Manchester connections of the temperance movement may have suggested his use of alcohol as an agent in the plot of *Hobson's Choice*. He obviously intends Hobson's single reference to temperance—he would like 'temperance young men' to marry his daughters—to be ironic at Hobson's expense. In addition, the doctor's moralistic comment that Hobson's complaint and character are the same is allowed to go unchallenged. The virtues of sobriety are more positively advanced in the opening of Act III where Brighouse's stage directions indicate that Maggie, Will, and their guests, are toasting the happy couple 'tea-cups in hand' after a meal 'at which tea only has been drunk'.

Dramatic method and construction

Brighouse's approach to play-writing was conditioned by plays he had seen. He was not a dramatist with a theory of drama, like Bertholt Brecht (1898–1956), or with a set of ideas he wished to dramatise, like Shaw. His pragmatic approach to drama is summed up in his statement that 'playgoing is the indispensable preliminary to play-writing' and that 'stageworthy plays are not written in ivory towers'. Brighouse treated play-writing as a craft which had to be learned. His own practice, as he pointed out in his autobiography, was to keep a play simple:

> I stood . . . dramatically, for simplicity of statement. Delving speculatively, I find origin for this in the plain living of my parents, combined possibly with boyhood attendance at a Congregational Church from which ritual was banished . . . In play-writing I put character first . . . But character must have something to it—in one word, plot . . .

This approach to subject matter also applied to the form Brighouse gave his plays. He admired craftsmanship and was not averse to using the traditional methods of constructing a play. There is a tendency among experimental writers to despise a 'well-made play' such as *Hobson's Choice* simply because it does rely on traditional devices. But the term 'well-made play' can only serve as a criticism where such techniques are used in a facile way, or to disguise the fact that a piece has little substance. Technique in *Hobson's Choice* is perfectly matched to the theme of the play, and cannot be regarded as meretricious.

The technique is responsible for the effectiveness of the play. Each act is subdivided into what may be regarded as scenes, marked by the exits and entrances of the various characters. Dramatic climaxes are skilfully developed where they will be most effective: at the end of the first act, for example. Hobson's drinking is used to make his fall into Beenstock's cellar less contrived, and the same is true of his final defeat at the hands of Will. Tension is maintained through Maggie's plan and the interest the audience takes in Will's development. Ironic reversals occur when Hobson changes from bully to servile tradesman when Mrs Hepworth enters his shop, or when Vickey's gushing concern for her sick father evaporates as soon as she finds out the full cost of sympathy for him. Finally, Brighouse's use of humour helps to unify the various parts of the play.

Brighouse also constructs *Hobson's Choice* around the repetition of actions and gestures—Maggie's continual insistence on her family's acceptance of Will as their equal is one example of this, as is the use of various folkloric elements. Chief among these is the scene in which Hobson's daughters are forced to say whether they will return to care for him or not. There are echoes of *King Lear* in the choice, and at one point Hobson actually refers to Maggie in Lear's own words as 'a thankless child'. But it is Maggie alone of the three sisters who passes the symbolic test, and Brighouse deliberately shifts the centre of gravity of the last act away from Hobson by giving the last words of the play to the triumphant and incredulous Will.

The three main turning-points in *Hobson's Choice* occur at the end of Act I, in Act III, and in Act IV. On each occasion, Hobson's authority is challenged and diminished. But, in order that it can be Will who makes the final and crucial challenge, Brighouse has to allow a year to lapse between Acts III and IV. In order to offset the slackening in dramatic tension this might cause, Brighouse concentrated the play's effect by using a small cast of characters and setting three of the four acts under Hobson's roof. In addition, Acts II and III take place on the same day, leading to a further concentration of action.

The characters of *Hobson's Choice*

Henry Hobson

Hobson is described on his first entry as 'fifty-five, successful, coarse, florid, and a parent of the period'. He is sure of nothing more than his own self-importance—an opinion he maintains until the very end of the play, when he pathetically agrees to an unequal partnership with Will. His most obvious failing is his excessive drinking, which leads him finally to alcoholism. Yet his downfall is not due simply to drink.

What Brighouse means by 'a parent of the period' is evident from Hobson's very first words. He does not talk to his daughters so much as lecture at them. He is very aggressive: the stage directions emphasise that his whole posture is hostile where they note that 'He takes a chair, straddling across it and facing them with his elbows on its back.' His manner of addressing his daughters is blunt to the point of being rude: 'I'm talking now, and you're listening,' he tells them. He also seems to have a very clear idea of his importance and status: 'I'm a decent-minded man. I'm Hobson. I'm British middle class and proud of it. I stand for commonsense and sincerity.'

It is evident at once that Hobson's sincerity is little more than a bluff. He pretends to be taken aback when his daughters assume that he is off to the Moonraker's, although it is obvious that this is his normal behaviour. While he is quite prepared to bully those in his power, he is servile with those who are wealthier and more influential than he is. In the comic confrontation with Mrs Hepworth in Act I, there is a sharp contrast between Hobson's threats to punish a workman for a misdemeanour which has not occurred and his fondling of Mrs Hepworth's foot. His attitude is both hypocritical and insincere, despite his earlier claims.

Hobson is also hypocritical in his attitude towards his business. He obviously feels that it would be foolish of him to pay wages for the work his daughters do, and yet he sees nothing wrong in spending his money on drink and neglecting his business. For the sake of business pride he is prepared to lie to his friend, Jim Heeler, about the length of time Mrs Hepworth has patronised his shop. He is blind to his own faults, sometimes comically so, as when he says that he would like his daughters to marry non-drinkers, just minutes before going off to the Moonraker's. Despite his self-confident tone, it is clear to the audience that he is not able to look after himself once his daughters have left him. Brighouse also cleverly suggests a parallel between Hobson's fall into the Beenstock cellar and his 'fall' in society; but he also makes it clear that decline had set in long before Maggie and Will left his shop.

Hobson's 'common-sense' is also a sham. He admits that Maggie is indispensable to his business when he tells Jim that although Alice and Vickey can be married off, 'Maggie's too useful to part with'. Similarly, after the encounter with Mrs Hepworth, it is equally apparent that Will is the other mainstay of his business. Yet he insists on treating both of them badly because of 'temper and obstinacy', as Tubby puts it. When they do leave, driven away by his behaviour, he blames them for his subsequent misfortunes in Act III. He refuses to admit the truth to himself.

Even the desertion of his daughters does not teach Hobson the error of his ways, as his ungenerous offer of Will's old job at his old wage shows.

At the point where he must have Maggie to look after him, he insists on taking her for granted. When Maggie reminds Hobson that her husband has a prior claim on her duty, he answers, 'I'll give him claims. Aren't I your father?' He believes he has a right to expect Maggie to give up her independence for the sake of his health. His attitude has not changed since the beginning of the first act, where he spoke of his daughters as if they were his personal property, to be used as unpaid labour and married off to men of his choosing. In reality he is too selfish to think of his daughters' happiness.

Hobson's blustering manner, however, fails to intimidate everyone he meets. When he encounters Dr MacFarlane we are aware that he has met his match, because the doctor is as stubborn as he is. Eventually it is a case of people having to defy Hobson in order to save him from the destructive consequences of his drinking and obstinacy. This is the role that the doctor, Maggie and Will play. Hobson's spirit has to be broken before there can be any improvement in his condition. However, not all of the humour in the play is at his expense, for he is given some of the funniest lines. Although we acquiesce in his downfall, we also pity him. Hobson's energy, his down-to-earth humour and vigorous use of Lancashire speech are always entertaining, and we may doubt, at the end of the play, that he will remain 'crushed-like' for ever.

Maggie Hobson

Although the title of the play uses Hobson's name, the most important character in it is Maggie. Not only does she manage to break free of her father and marry against his wishes, but she organises the lives of most of the other characters in the play. Even professional people, like Albert, have to fall in with Maggie's plans. She is single-minded and persuasive, and she knows what she wants. It is this quality which marks her off from everyone else in the play. In Act II, Alice questions Maggie's tactics: 'I don't know what you're aiming at, Maggie, but—.' Maggie interrupts her, and draws this crucial distinction between them: 'The difference between us is that I do. I always did.' By convincing first Will, then Albert, Alice, Vickey and Freddy that she has a plan, she manages to turn the tables on Hobson.

Maggie's determination to succeed often makes her appear ruthless, even slightly unsympathetic. In her proposal to Will in the first act, she answers his 'I wish you'd leave me alone' with the retort 'So does the fly when the spider catches him.' This is a good joke, but it is a sharp one, and the image it gives is of Maggie as a predator. In the ensuing scene with Ada Figgins we may also find her ousting of Will's fiancée rather harsh. There is a touch of ruthlessness in her advice to the departing Ada to part quickly and without crying about it. However, it is soon apparent that Maggie's scheming is beneficial when Will endorses her plans for rescuing him from the clutches of Mrs Figgins with his comment, 'It's like an 'appy dream. Eh, Maggie, you do manage things.' In her plans against Hobson she could be accused of using blackmail. But it is Hobson who puts himself in the position where he can be taken advantage of because of his pride and self-importance. It is his neglect of business and drinking which bring about his accident, just as it is his exaggerated sense of his own importance which makes him take fright at the possibility of a court case. Similarly, during the course of the next three acts, it becomes clear that Maggie's intervention is for the benefit of those involved. She has to be tough because those around her are in awe of Hobson and would do nothing to help themselves without her prompting.

Maggie's organisational ability is obvious from the start. Her handling of Albert when he tries to speak with Alice in the first act shows us her talent as a saleswoman, and this is confirmed by Mrs Hepworth's appeal to her as the only sensible person present. She is not the only one who turns to Maggie for advice. In Act III Hobson wishes to consult her over his legal difficulties, even though she has left his shop and taken Will with her. In Act IV it is Maggie whom Dr MacFarlane prescribes for Hobson's cure; like the other characters in the play, he defers to her reputation for organising people. Finally even Hobson himself has to acknowledge her supremacy, although by this stage it is shared with Will.

Maggie's triumph is perhaps most evident in her treatment of Will. Her proposal to him is something she has planned beforehand, and although she declares, 'I've got the love alright', it is the business aspect of the partnership which predominates at this point. Her great achievement is to make an equal of Will, turning him from a weakling into the strongest man in the play, one who can dominate a joint business with Hobson. In the course of this coaching of Will, Maggie develops herself, although to a lesser extent. She becomes less sharp and authoritarian as her responsibilities are gradually shared with Will.

Brighouse gives several opportunities for the actress playing Maggie to show the natural warmth of her character. There is an early awareness that the marriage is intended as more than a business arrangement in her description of it to Hobson in Act I as 'the strangest, finest match'. Again there is no practical need for her to arrange her sisters' marriages, yet she does so. Her hardness is also offset by the sentiment she displays in pressing one of Mrs Hepworth's hot-house flowers in her Bible as a souvenir.

Despite her defiance of her father, Maggie does not believe in overturning social conventions. Her rebellion is based on common sense rather than feminist fervour. She is firmly committed to the traditional values of marriage and hard work, and educates Will to the point where he can be 'gaffer' in their home. Moreover, she is the only one of the three sisters who is prepared to accept her duty to look after their father. This involves a sacrifice of some of her hard-earned independence. It is a sacrifice Maggie is prepared to make because independence was only ever a means to an end for her, the end being a normal and prosperous married life.

Although Hobson's claim to represent common sense and traditional values is shown to be bogus, it should not be forgotten that Maggie takes after him in several ways. She too is forceful, in command of the pithy colloquial phrase, and suspicious of doctors and lawyers. Part of the interest felt in the outcome of the play is a result of our sensing the similarity of temperament of its two main antagonists.

Will Mossop

Will is the character who develops most during the course of *Hobson's Choice*, and who presents the greatest challenge to an actor in the play. Brighouse deliberately presents him first at his most unattractive. His unkempt appearance and his emergence from the cellar combine to reinforce the impression of someone who is downtrodden. His subterranean existence and his shy, unambitious nature are summed up in Mrs Hepworth's exclamation 'He's like a rabbit' when he dives back down through the trap-door. But the stage directions also describe Will as having potentialities, and it is these which Maggie sees and strives to develop.

In the first discussion between him and Maggie we are given some indications that Will is not completely humble. In part, Maggie's tactics are to challenge Will's lack of ambition and goad him into showing some spirit. She tells him that he is a natural genius at boot-making, but a natural fool at everything else. He does not defend himself against this insult. A few lines later, Maggie goes even further, calling him a fool for his lack of ambition. Will's retort 'Then I'm a loyal fool' is the beginning of his self-assertion. Later on he declares plainly that he is not in love with Maggie, and drops some of his deferential attitude by calling her 'Maggie' rather than 'Miss Maggie'. Brighouse makes Will's growth believable because it is uneven, just as it would be in real life. When Ada Figgins enters the shop soon afterwards, Will becomes his old helpless self again, making comments which are both pathetic and humorous, while pleading with Ada to fight for him.

Despite his backwardness, Will is a likeable character almost from the beginning of the play. Apart from Alice and Vickey, who are snobbish where Will is concerned, most of the other characters are quick to admit Will's endearing nature. Even Hobson, who describes him as the son of 'a workhouse brat. A come-by-chance', has to admit that he has nothing against him personally. Later, when Hobson does have something against Will, he is prepared to say, 'You're a backward lad, but you know your trade and it's an honest one.' Although this is slightly patronising praise, it is confirmed by the way Tubby, Albert and Freddy treat Will. He has a humanising influence on Maggie during the course of the play; it is also

Will who tries to make peace with Alice and Vickey when Hobson dismisses them from his home, and who feels sorry for Hobson at the end of Act IV.

Acts II and III take place only a month after Will and Maggie have left Hobson's, and we would not expect Will to have changed much in that space of time. Brighouse carefully shows the unevenness of his hero's progress. For example, he makes Maggie say that she does not trust him when Will tells her that he has put a sign on their door, in Act III. This gives us an indication of how far Will has progressed in Maggie's estimation. But at the beginning of the same act, we find Will making a speech which impresses the guests at the wedding-feast. Although he falters once, and has been coached by Maggie, it is a sign that he has made progress since the first act. By cleverly placing Will's writing lesson at the end of the act, Brighouse also leads us to expect further advances from Will, and these are amply demonstrated in Act IV.

The last act complete's Will's transformation from comic, slow-witted menial to master of the situation. The comedy is no longer at Will's expense, but as a result of the reversal of roles. Although he gives Maggie most of the credit for the triumph over Hobson, it is really his personal victory—a victory over his arrogant former employer, but more importantly over himself and his circumstances.

Alice Hobson

Alice is the middle daughter in the Hobson family. Like Vickey, the youngest daughter, she is self-centred and snobbish. She sees marriage to Albert Prosser as a way of rising in society and escaping from the work she has to do at Hobson's shop. Even when she is at the shop, however, she spends her time knitting, as the stage directions for Act I indicate. After Maggie has left, the opening of Act II sees her in charge of the shop while Hobson is out, and making a mess of things. She cannot give Tubby orders, and she is unable to manage the simple arithmetic required for filling in a ledger.

Alice is slightly more independent and assertive than Vickey, as the elder of the two sisters. Nevertheless, she is no match for Maggie and cannot stand up to Hobson except on minor issues, such as clothing. This is shown in the first act, where she lectures her father on fashion. Later, in Act III, she shows her domination of Albert when she stops him making a speech after Will's. However, she is defeated in the argument with Will in Act IV when he reminds her and Vickey of the help he and Maggie gave them by arranging their marriage-portions. Like Vickey, Alice is guilty of ingratitude towards her sister and brother-in-law.

Alice's snobbery is connected with her desire to be the wife of a fashionable young lawyer. Before her marriage she shows disdain for Will in Act

I, telling Maggie that she will not acknowledge Will as her brother-in-law. After her marriage, in Act IV, her sense of superiority has increased, and she is described as 'languidly haughty'. She tries to treat Will as her social inferior by ordering him around. Her pretensions, however, are deflated by Maggie and Will when they point out the realities of the situation.

Vickey Hobson

Vickey is the youngest of the Hobson sisters. Brighouse distinguishes her from Alice, whose dramatic function is identical, by making her prettier and also more emotional than Alice. We are given the impression that since she is the baby of the family she has probably been spoiled a little. Her gushing greeting of Hobson in Act IV is an example of this. In her self-centredness and snobbery, however, she is like Alice.

It is Vickey who is most concerned about Hobson's criticism of bustles in the first act. She knows that despite his criticism, Hobson is proud of her good looks. Like Alice, she is prepared to stand up to her father only on relatively minor issues, such as dress. Hobson sums up her attempts to get round him by saying, 'Vickey, you're pretty, but you can lie like a gas-meter.'

If anything, Vickey is even more impractical than Alice. At the beginning of Act II, Alice is at least attempting to do some work in the shop, whereas Vickey is simply sitting behind the counter, reading. She argues with Alice and shows her complete lack of interest in the shop by commenting 'That's your look-out' to Alice's perfectly reasonable question. Like Alice, she remains a snob, and she has a slightly nastier, more spiteful tongue than her sister. This is apparent in Act IV with her comment that 'Will Mossop hasn't the spirit of a louse', and her later witticism 'Beggars on horseback'. She is prepared to believe the worst of other people, judging them by her own nature. This is particularly clear in the last act, when she is alone with Alice. Alice is not quite as ready to see possibly base motives in the actions of Maggie and Will, and Vickey has to spell things out for her, pointing out that Hobson might leave all or most of his money to Maggie and Will.

For Vickey, Freddy Beenstock is a chance to escape the world of Hobson's shop. Like Alice, she is snobbish about her husband's occupation. She is indignant when Will points out that Freddy is in trade, asserting her social superiority by making a distinction between wholesale business and trade. At the end of the play she shows the shallowness of her affection for her father by refusing to return and nurse him because she is expecting a baby.

Albert Prosser

Albert is from a section of the middle class superior to the Hobsons, since he and his father live by the law rather than by 'trade'. However, when we first encounter him, he is routed by Maggie, and is afraid of meeting Hobson in his capacity as Alice's suitor. He resembles the girls in his concern about social status, and is embarrassed at the prospect of having to take Will's and Maggie's furniture to their new home. Appropriately, it is Albert's pride which makes him the perfect match for the snobbish Alice.

Albert also matches Alice in his concern for money and possessions. He shows greediness in his attempt to get Hobson to settle the case brought against him for a thousand pounds. Maggie comments drily on his ability to advance his own interests, and forces him to ask for half the amount. Here she demonstrates a better grasp of the law than Albert, but he is generally good at his work and sharp-witted. It is Albert, for example, who notices the hot-house flowers at the wedding-feast and who asks where Will and Maggie got the money with which to set up their business. He also likes the sound of his own voice, appropriately enough for a lawyer, but it is clear even at the wedding-feast that Alice will rule him when she prevents him making another speech. Like Freddy's, his opinions will not amount to much with his wife; Vickey speaks for both sisters when she tells Maggie that she and Alice do not need to ask their husbands.

Freddy Beenstock

Freddy plays a less important part in the play than Albert Prosser. He is the son of a neighbouring tradesman, the exact social equal of Vickey despite her later protestations that her husband is not involved in trade. He shows a certain amount of tactfulness when he tells the girls about their father's accident, saying that their father 'wasn't looking very carefully' when he fell into the Beenstock cellar. Like Albert, Vickey and Alice, he is forced into co-operating with Maggie's plans. When Albert raises objections to helping with the washing-up after the wedding-feast, Freddy is firm with him, pointing out their need of Maggie's help. He is realistic, seeing that it is necessary to give way to Maggie if she is to arrange marriage portions for her sisters.

As a character, Freddy is not as fully drawn as Albert. His dramatic function is the most prominent thing about him. He is needed because Vickey must have a suitor, and because the case against Hobson must be brought by someone who knows the family well enough to fall in with Maggie's plans. Insofar as he does have a distinct character, he is shown to be subordinate to Albert, who gives him his orders during the washing-up scene, although he insists on doing as Maggie wishes when Albert grumbles. It is also Freddy who gently mocks Will for being afraid of being left alone with his wife.

Mrs Hepworth

Although Mrs Hepworth only appears on stage once during the play, her invisible presence is felt several times because it is she who lends Will and

Maggie the money to set up their business. Without her, their independence would not have been possible.

As the only upper-class character in the play, Mrs Hepworth conforms to dramatic conventions by being domineering and outspoken. Her virtue is her ability to see through pretension and to value fine workmanship. She dismisses the fawning Hobson with comic brutality, finally telling him to be quiet, and gives the first hint of what will happen in the play when she queries Hobson's assurance that Will will not change his place of employment and suggests that Hobson underpays him. She also remembers Maggie as a sensible person, which confirms her ability to judge character. Although there is something of the Fairy Godmother in her patronage of Will and Maggie, Brighouse reduces the improbability of her behaviour by indicating that she backs them because she sees them as a good business investment. Her shrewdness is borne out in the last act when Will happens to mention to Hobson that he has repaid his debt to Mrs Hepworth. Despite her condescension and high-handedness in dealing with people, Mrs Hepworth's virtues outweigh her brusque manner.

Timothy Wadlow ('Tubby')

Tubby is the foreman bootmaker at Hobson's shop. He is described as a small, old man 'in dingy clothes with no collar', without a coat. The lack of a collar and coat indicates a lowly social status, and Tubby's nature fits his appearance.

Although he is in a position of authority, his subservience to members of the Hobson family is complete and is shown in the opening of the second act. He is prepared to offer comments on the state of the business, but not to take responsibility for any decisions. His lack of initiative is demonstrated in the comment: 'When you've told me what to do, I'll use my intelligence and see it's done properly.'

Tubby is foreman because of his seniority rather than because of his skill. He does not have Will's natural talent for making boots, although he taught Will the trade. He is, however, loyal to Hobson after his daughters have left him. He is also able to see clearly what is happening to Hobson's business. In Act II he notes the steep decline of high-class trade in Hobson's shop, and in Act IV he says that Hobson's bad temper and his obstinacy are ruining his business. Loyalty is Tubby's strongest character trait, despite his grumbling that cooking Hobson's breakfast is no work for a foreman, and his complaints to Jim Heeler.

Jim Heeler

Jim is a grocer, Hobson's boon companion at the Moonraker's, and the friend to whom Hobson pours out all his troubles. The two men are similar in many ways, holding the same opinions on the place of women and having the same taste for drink. Jim is more restrained than Hobson, urging moderation on him in his treatment of his daughters. He points out that in order to marry them off, he will have to provide dowries — a point which Hobson had overlooked.

Jim also flatters Hobson, knowing his weakness for praise, and compares his oratory to that of John Bright. This is too strong even for Hobson, who points out with unconscious irony that a 'good case needs no flattery' just after he has been flattering Mrs Hepworth. Jim comically modifies this praise to calling Hobson the best debater at the Moonraker's, a title which Hobson accepts. The scene shows how the two men pay each other compliments and confirm each other's opinions. Jim is as fond of down-to-earth aphorisms as Hobson, using phrases such as 'it's steel in a man's character that subdues the women.'

Like Tubby, Jim is loyal to Hobson, although in a different way. He is unwilling to listen to Tubby's criticism of Hobson, partly because Tubby is an employee and should not be encouraged to be critical of his master. We feel that he is a good friend to Hobson, but he encourages the heavy drinking which brings about Hobson's downfall. He is ineffectual in the last act, and, although he tries to defend Hobson against Dr MacFarlane, he is dismissed. Although he is Hobson's friend, he can have no role to play in saving Hobson because, in a sense, he is part of Hobson's problem.

Ada Figgins

Ada only appears once in the play, and this is deliberate since Brighouse does not want the audience to get to know her well enough to sympathise with her. He also tries to make us side with Maggie, despite her harsh treatment of Ada, by making Ada 'weak, poor-blooded and poor-spirited' in his stage directions. He insists, however, that she should not appear ridiculous because this would lower our estimation of Will, and because Maggie must at least encounter some opposition.

Ada is naïve, thinking at first that Maggie is congratulating Will and her on their engagement, and she is pathetically grateful for Maggie's attention. She is also honest and frank in her replies to Maggie's questions. When Maggie mocks Will, she defends him openly as 'the lad I love'. But she soon gives up her defence of her right to Will, and she is described as acting stupidly and weakly. Her comment 'It's daylight robbery' marks the point at which she admits defeat.

Much of our sympathy for Ada is dispelled by the way in which she falls back on the threat of her mother in order to make Will conform. We are further alienated from her when we learn that Ada's mother played a big part in making the match. Will himself obviously feels relieved at being freed from the clutches of Mrs Figgins. By this time Ada has served her dramatic function, which is to offer a minor but realistic obstacle to Maggie's plans, and to allow Brighouse to exploit the comedy of a situation in which two women fight over a single man.

Doctor MacFarlane

Upon his entrance, the doctor is described as 'a domineering Scotsman of fifty'. During the consultation with Hobson, he forces his patient to listen to him or sit down on several occasions. He also dismisses Jim Heeler, who refuses to keep quiet during the consultation. It is necessary for the doctor to be as forceful as he is because he and Maggie and Will must break Hobson's obstinate and self-destructive attitude.

There is little variation in the tone of the doctor's conversation. More than any other character in the play, he verges on being a stock theatrical type. He soon begins a battle of wills with Hobson. Hobson, who has met his match, ironically refers to the doctor as a bully, and decides to teach him a lesson. An extra edge is given to the confrontation by the fact that Hobson regards the doctor as 'a foreigner'. At one point, the doctor decides to abandon Hobson to his fate, but then changes his mind. He is even more obstinate than Hobson himself, and refuses to take his money and be dismissed. The doctor's most violent outburst is shown by his lapse into a thicker Scottish accent. However, unlike Hobson, he never quite forgets his manners.

Language and style

One of the most vital contributions made by the regional drama, of which *Hobson's Choice* is one of the best examples, was the expressive power of regional speech. Before the Repertory Movement, local accent and dialect in drama were usually treated as something inherently ridiculous. It was part of Brighouse's task as a playwright, as he saw it, to change that attitude. Along with other dramatists of the time, he helped to make the theatre aware of the possibilities of local speech. Playwrights such as J.M. Synge (1871–1909) and Sean O'Casey (1884–1964) used this shift in tastes to introduce more realism and energy into dialogue which, until a short while before, had been dominated by the refined speech of the upper and upper-middle classes in the plays of dramatists such as Shaw and Oscar Wilde. The latest variation on this interest in regional accents and manners is to be seen today in the wide regional variety of television 'soap operas' — *Brookside*, *Emmerdale Farm*, *Crossroads*, *Coronation Street* and *Eastenders*.

In order to understand the way Brighouse uses Lancashire speech in *Hobson's Choice*, we need first of all to distinguish between dialect, which includes words and phrases which are peculiar to a particular area, and accent, which is simply the local pronunciation of the language. Some of

Brighouse's plays, such as *Lonesome-like* (1909), contain more dialect than *Hobson's Choice*. Brighouse's play *The Price of Coal* was even 'translated' from Lancashire into Lanarkshire dialect for a performance at Glasgow Repertory Theatre. But difficulties of dialect are not great in *Hobson's Choice*, although the play does demand that it be spoken in a Salford, or at least Lancashire, accent.

The attitude of some London playgoers to the strongly regional flavour of his play is revealed in a story of Brighouse's. During one of the many London productions of *Hobson's Choice* he overheard a lady at the box-office of the theatre ask if the actress currently playing Maggie (the famous Edyth Goodall) came from Lancashire. 'Oh, no!' was the reply. 'She is really quite English!' What the person in the box-office was referring to was probably the dialect usage in *Hobson's Choice*. There is not really much of it. Most of it is made up of Northern expressions — 'nobbut', 'owt', 'happen', 'summat'. Some of these amount to whole phrases — 'You'll come, *so what* he says', where 'so what' means 'whatever'. There is also the use (although not consistent) of the second person singular 'thou' and 'thee' in the play. It is an intimate or patronising form of 'you' which standard English has lost, but which is found in many other languages (French 'tu' and German 'du'). Sometimes the definite article 'the' is shortened to t', or omitted altogether, as in Hobson's 'At moment I'm on uppishness.' There are also usages which would be considered ungrammatical in standard English, such as Maggie's double negative 'no use to nobody'.

What *Hobson's Choice* most gains from Lancashire speech is better described as its style. The down-to-earth bluntness of Hobson and Maggie in particular gives the play's dialogue liveliness and memorability; the local speech of the characters is responsible for many rough aphorisms and much of the humour. Hobson uses such phrases in order to tell his home truths: 'Your penny buns 'ull cost you tuppence now — and more,' he warns Freddy and Albert. His suspicion of lawyers is summed up in 'Honest men live by business and lawyers live by the law.' Often a succession of short sentences indicate the terse, blunt delivery the actor must adopt, as in Hobson's 'Question was whether the razor would beat me, or I'd beat razor. I won, that time. The razor's in the yard. But I'll never dare to try shaving myself again.' Such a style fits what we know of Hobson's character and the situation in which he finds himself. Maggie's uncompromising character also shows itself in her style of speech. Her comment 'They're always out of someone's stock' is an example, as is her summary of her sisters' unwillingness to look after their father in Act IV. When affection is shown, at the end of the play, it is in an almost inarticulate manner: 'Eh, lad,' says Maggie, to which Will's response is 'Eh, lass!' Like the forthrightness of much of the rest of the dialogue, such language perfectly suits the slightly dour but warm-hearted nature of the play and its characters.

Part 4

Hints for study

Studying the play

Reading a play is, in a sense, experiencing it at one remove. *Hobson's Choice* was written with theatrical performance in mind, and some of its effect will be lost unless you try to visualise the text as a play while you are reading it. Try to calculate how an audience would react to moments of humour or confrontation; read the play with other students in order to understand the interaction of the characters more fully; discuss problems of staging, perhaps even reconstructing the layout of each set from the stage directions, using a model; try to work out exactly the movements of the characters around the stage when they are on it. If possible, of course, you should try to see the play being performed. Although the script of the film version of *Hobson's Choice* was not approved by Brighouse it is also well worth trying to see the film, on video if possible, because it will help you see the period background and setting of the play more clearly in your mind's eye.

While you are studying the play, pay attention to plot, structure, characterisation, themes and language. You must know precisely what happens in each act, and how Brighouse has broken it down into separate scenes. Try to identify the climax of each scene or act, and work out major turning-points in the action. Ask yourself why the playwright has made the characters do this or that. Decide which elements of a scene follow on from what went before, and which are being used to prepare us for what is to come. Work out other ways in which the playwright might have stressed the continuity of the play's events: the parallel of Mrs Hepworth's card and Will's, for example, in Acts I and II. Always remember that this play, like any other, is an artificial creation. The more you understand of its construction details, the more you will be able to appreciate its overall effect.

Answering questions on the play

All criticism of literature is subjective, and there is no necessarily 'right' answer as there may be in mathematics or the sciences. Nevertheless, any answer you make must be logically argued and well illustrated by reference to, or direct quotation from, the text. It is not good enough simply to assert what you feel in an essay about the play. Your teacher or examiner is not marking you according to the strength of your convictions; he or she is more interested in the way in which you present your argument.

Before answering a question, think about what is required to answer it. What is the examiner or teacher trying to get out of you? You should then spend time—even in an examination—sketching out your answer before you start writing. Use scrap paper and, if you are in an examination, remember that it is better to spend five minutes at this stage than to realise at the end of the examination that you have left out vital information because you did not plan your answer. Your essay should contain no more than half a dozen main points, and have about as many paragraphs. It should have a structure—a beginning, a middle and an end. Each point you make should be backed up by reference to the play. One way to construct an answer is to take issue with the question, particularly if it asks you whether you agree or disagree with a statement. You may or may not have a preference in such a case, but you should give both sides of the argument and, in conclusion, state your own position. This should be seen to be the only logical position to take from the way you have presented your arguments and information.

However you decide to write your essay, always bear the reader and the question in mind. How much information is required to prove a point? More than two or three examples will probably be superfluous, and in an examination will be a waste of valuable time. You must prove to the reader that you are familiar with the play, but you should avoid simply telling the story. You should assume the reader to have a certain minimum knowledge of the play. Test everything you have written by referring it back to the question each time you complete a paragraph. Does it help to answer the question? Is it relevant to the arguments you are making?

Do not repeat yourself; each part of your answer should contain new information. Above all, be specific. If you base your answer on individual incidents and characters rather than on general ideas, you will steer clear of vagueness and the temptation to give the story of the play.

Review questions

---

(1) The theatrical background to *Hobson's Choice*

(a) Who and what were the major theatrical influences on Harold Brighouse's practice as a playwright?

(b) Give an account of the Repertory Movement and assess its significance.

(c) Would it be accurate to call *Hobson's Choice* a comedy in the classical tradition?

---

(2) Brighouse's stagecraft in *Hobson's Choice*

(a) Discuss in detail what we learn from the stage directions at the beginning of each act. Write a paragraph on the setting of each act.

(b) Break down each act into its main 'scenes'.

(c) Locate the main climaxes of each act.

(d) Explain why Brighouse chooses not to include the following possible scenes in his play: Hobson discussing his problems with Jim Heeler at the Moonraker's; Maggie and Will being married in church; Maggie and Will asking Mrs Hepworth to lend the money for Will's business.

(e) Write a short essay on the use of coincidence in the plot.

(f) Examine in detail the proposal scene between Will and Maggie in Act I, and one scene from each of the other three acts. How theatrically effective are they? In each case describe how events and dialogue contribute to the overall dramatic effect. Pay attention to stage directions and the movement of the characters involved.

(3) Themes

(a) Discuss the attitude to work of the main characters in *Hobson's Choice*.

(b) How do differences of class affect the way the characters in the play treat each other?

(c) 'Women are worse than men for getting above themselves,' Jim Heeler tells Hobson. What are the attitudes of the male characters in the play to the women in it?

(d) Would it be true to say that women ultimately dominate men in *Hobson's Choice*?

(e) Explain the role that drinking plays in the development of the events of the play.

(f) *Hobson's Choice* is subtitled 'A Lancashire Comedy in Four Acts'. Why did Brighouse insist on the play being set in Lancashire?

(g) Write an essay on the use of regional language in the play. How does such language add to its impact on the stage?

(h) 'The theme of the play can be summed up as "Pride comes before a fall".' How true is this statement?

(4) Characters

(a) Discuss the similarities between Maggie and her father. What weaknesses and strengths do they share?

(b) Is the breaking of Hobson's spirit in Act IV convincing? How is the audience prepared for it?

(c) 'I'm a decent-minded man . . . I stand for common-sense and sincerity.' How accurate is Hobson's own assessment of his character?

(d) Write an essay dealing with the role of the minor characters in *Hobson's Choice* (that is, all but the members of Hobson's family and Will Mossop); *or* write a paragraph each about four of the following:

Albert Prosser; Tubby Wadlow; Freddy Beenstock; Jim Heeler; Ada Figgins; Mrs Hepworth.

(e) Describe how Will Mossop changes during the course of the play. How correct is Vickey to say he 'hasn't the spirit of a louse' in Act IV?

(f) Is Maggie a bully? Illustrate your answer with examples of the way she organises the lives of others, and of the softer side of her nature.

(g) Write an essay explaining the reasons why Alice and Vickey have a snobbish attitude towards Will. Do other characters share their attitude? How does Maggie try to make her family accept Will?

(h) 'You're a business idea in the shape of a man.' How well does Maggie's description of Will sum up their relationship? Explain how it changes, and why.

Study questions

The following questions are designed to help you in your revision of the play:

Act I

(1) Discuss Hobson's use of the word 'uppishness' and his reasons for using it.

(2) What do we learn about the status of women in Act I?

(3) Are we prepared for Maggie's proposal to Will? If so, how?

(4) Analyse the reasons Hobson gives both for and against the marriage of his daughters.

(5) Write a summary of the events and changes in attitude of the characters from the time Alice and Vickey leave Maggie alone with their father to the end of Act I.

Act II

(1) Describe the condition of the shop and the way it is run one month after Maggie and Will have left it.

(2) Examine the scene between Maggie's and Freddy's entry and the point when Freddy is sent out to fetch Albert. Compare and contrast the different attitudes to Maggie's plans, and examine the way Maggie treats her sisters.

(3) What does Maggie mean by the phrase 'They're always out of someone's stock'?

(4) What *dramatic* reasons might Brighouse have for keeping Hobson out of the whole of Act II?

(5) How does Maggie persuade the others — her sisters, their suitors, and Will — to follow her plans?

Act III

---

(1) Examine the stage settings for Act III very carefully. Make a note of *everything* they tell you about the characters in the play.

(2) Read the scene in which Freddy, Albert and Will are washing up together after the wedding-feast. What do you learn from it about the attitudes of the young men?

(3) How does Maggie manage to make Hobson accept her marriage to Will, and accept him as her husband?

(4) Which aspects of the threatened court case upset Hobson most?

(5) The scene in which Maggie takes Will into the bedroom by his ear could be described as farcical. Explain why you think it might succeed or fail in a production of the play.

Act IV

---

(1) Examine the scene from Hobson's entrance to the appearance of Doctor MacFarlane. Is Hobson just feeling sorry for himself, or is he really ill?

(2) Explain the ways in which the doctor forces Hobson to obey him.

(3) By what means do Vickey and Alice try to oppose Maggie and Will?

(4) 'You've no *right* to expect I care whether you sink or swim.' Is Will correct in this assessment of his duty to Hobson?

(5) What differences of opinion are there between Will and Maggie in Act IV?

Illustrative quotations

While you must have a full understanding of the plot, themes, characters and structure of the play, you should also have quotations ready to illustrate your argument. You should select quotations which are relevant. It is wise not to use one without comment; it should be clear to your reader why you are using it. Nor should quotations be overused; nor must you let your response to a question be determined too much by certain quotations which you know. However, if you can construct your answer so that it includes relevant quotations, you should do so.

For examination purposes, it may be useful to learn six usefully illustrative quotations from each act. Study the significance and the context of the following passages:

Act I

'I'm a decent-minded man . . . diligence of the working-classes' (pp.6–7). This is Hobson's response to Vickey and Alice when they are both arguing with him about their desire to be allowed to dress fashionably.

'Do you know what keeps this business on its legs? . . . We're a pair, Will Mossop' (p.15). Maggie uses business logic as she begins her proposal to Will.

'It's news to me we're snobs in Salford' (p.23). However, the rest of Maggie's family *are* snobs.

'I'm none wanting thy Maggie . . . stick to her like glue' (p.25). This is Will's reaction to Hobson's threat. But Hobson *does* hit him, and Will responds by kissing Maggie. It is a turning-point in the play.

Act II

Identify the context and explain the significance of the following quotations:

TUBBY: The high-class trade has dropped . . . clogs for stock if you like (p.26).

MAGGIE: He's in the family . . . respectful to my Willie (p.30).

ALBERT: I've made this out to your instructions . . . going into court with it (p.36).

WILLIE: Yes, Maggie . . . I'll toe the line with you (p.38).

Act III

'He'll do . . . thought most of at the Bank' (p.40). This prediction of Maggie's is made before Will becomes Hobson's partner.

'I look at it like this . . . nuisance to us all our lives' (p.42). Albert says this to Freddy when they are left to do the washing-up with Will.

'I'll run that shop . . . I've got to thank for this' (p.55). This is Hobson's reaction to learning that he has been 'diddled'.

'I thought I'd press it in my Bible . . . reminded of this day' (p.58). Pay close attention to the stage directions here.

Act IV

'I'm dirty now . . . I'd have cut my throat' (p.63). This is Hobson's description of his battle with himself. Although the account is serious, his self-pity also makes it very amusing.

'Your complaint and your character are the same' (p.65). This is Doctor MacFarlane's moralistic comment on Hobson's illness.

'I'm doing well . . . don't try interference on with me' (p.79). Will is speaking in continuation of the proposal he makes to Hobson, after his interruption of it.

'Did I? . . . he's the old master, and—' (p.81). To begin with, Will cannot believe in his victory over Hobson.

Sample answers

---

1. How does *Hobson's Choice* succeed as a comedy?

Hobson's Choice succeeds mainly as a comedy of reversal in which Will Mossop, the downtrodden, abject boot-hand of Act I, overcomes his former master and becomes the dominant partner in his business by the end of the play. The structure of the play is based on a series of confrontations in which the power and authority of Hobson are diminished, and Will's final triumph is made realistic and believable to the audience because of the lapse of thirteen months between Acts I and IV.

Brighouse is also successful in exploiting the conventions of romantic comedy for their humorous potential. In the scene involving Maggie, Will and Ada Figgins, for example, two women fight for the right to marry the man they both love. This is a deliberate inversion of the usual situation in which two men fight over a woman. What is more, Will is reduced to a pathetically comic and helpless figure during the struggle, only capable of feeble protestations.

Such anti-romantic comedy is complemented by Maggie's down-to-earth dry humour, as when she compares courting to the buckle on a fancy slipper. Brighouse uses Maggie's dominant role in the play to provide a series of comic moments. Sometimes her deflating remarks are comic in themselves, as in the scene where Alice is shocked by her choice of a˙brass wedding-ring taken from stock. Maggie's reply 'They're always out of someone's stock' pokes fun at her sister's outrage and concern for appearances. At other times, Maggie contrives comic scenes as part of her plans. When she forces her sisters to kiss Will, and her father to eat a slice of wedding-cake, we realise that she has the serious intention of making her family accept Will. Nevertheless, these actions are also a source of comedy.

Hobson's Choice contains several characters who are inherently comic. Hobson excites laughter because of the way his words and deeds contradict his image of himself as standing for 'common-sense and decency'. Whilst he is prepared to bully his daughters, he immediately adopts a servile tone when the upper-class Mrs Hepworth enters his shop. When she leaves, he again changes his attitude, declaring that he will not permit her to enter his shop ever again. His attitude changes yet again when he sees the opportunity to boast to his friend Jim Heeler that Mrs Hepworth is an old customer. These changes all take place within a very short space of time, and Hobson's inconsistency is shown up in a comic light.

Brighouse manages to vary the comic effect of the play considerably. He supplements comic characters and situations with the comic expressiveness of Lancashire speech, and in the last scene of Act III he creates humour without words at all. As Maggie silently leads Will into the bedroom by his ear the audience will be made to smile, rather than laugh, at a situation which is both farcical and moving. This variety of comic tone adds to the power of the overall comic effect of the play.

In the final act, the revelation of Hobson's alcoholism is made comic by his self-pity which prevents us from taking his plight too seriously. It prepares us for the fine comedy of Hobson's confrontation with Will, in which he is finally beaten. As in classical comedy, an anti-social figure is discomfited and humbled, much to the amusement of the audience. But Brighouse is careful to soften the harshness of his comedy by saving Hobson from absolute humiliation, and by giving the good-natured Will the play's last words of comic incongruity, 'Well, by gum!'

---

2. Discuss the reasons for Hobson's downfall.

The main reason for Hobson's downfall is his growing taste for drink, which finally leads to his being given six months to live, unless he changes his ways. His drinking leads to his fall into Beenstock's cellar and allows Maggie to put her plan into operation. It also reduces Hobson to an alcoholic and allows Will to triumph over him in Act IV. However, Hobson's fall is also the result of his pride and arrogance or, as Dr MacFarlane puts it, his 'complaint and . . . character are the same'. These vices mark him out immediately as a character the audience wishes to see taken down a peg or two. They excuse the actions the other characters feel forced to take against him.

On his first appearance we see Hobson bully his daughters when they challenge his statement that he is going out for a quarter of an hour only, even though they are right in assuming that he is off to the Moonraker's. He treats them as his own property, and he is shown to be mean when he tells Jim Heeler that he would be a fool to pay them wages. It appears that he only gives them money for clothes because he likes to see them well dressed, thinks their smart appearance is good for the business, and strongly objects when Alice and Vickey buy dresses with bustles. He is also very aggrieved when Mrs Hepworth implies that he underpays Will, his best boot-hand. His meanness is responsible for his retraction of a promise to marry his daughters off when he finds out that he will have to pay marriage-settlements.

Hobson's treatment of Maggie and Will starts the series of events which will lead to his downfall. They are initially prepared to work for him if he will pay Maggie a wage and let them marry. His refusal on both points drives them into leaving and setting up a rival business. Hobson, however, is blind to his mistakes. In Act III he blames all his misfortunes on Maggie and Will. In the same act he attacks Maggie for tricking him out of the five hundred pounds which will enable his daughters to marry and leave his shop. But his claims are hypocritical since he was drinking heavily before

Maggie and Will left, as well as neglecting his business. He fails to see that his daughters have a right to a life of their own and makes his plight worse by blaming everyone but himself for his problems.

Evidence that the desertion of Maggie and Will need not have affected Hobson's business too badly comes from Tubby's statement to Jim Heeler at the beginning of Act IV, when he declares that Hobson's business would have survived Will's competition, had care and tact been used. Tubby implies that if Hobson had paid his daughters a wage and treated them with tact they might still be working in the shop. As it is, Hobson has hired male assistants who are unsuitable for the high-class female customers the business requires. Tubby, too, puts the blame on Hobson's obstinacy and his bad temper.

Hobson's most public vice is that favourite of Victorian melodrama, 'the demon drink'. Yet alcoholism also symbolises his other faults. His actual drunkenness corresponds to a moral and social drunkenness, an inability to think or act in a sober, rational manner. Because he is drunk with pride and self-importance he brings about his own downfall. It is both ironic and appropriate that the people who force him to make 'Hobson's Choice' — Maggie and Will — are the people he first drove away by his behaviour.

---

3. Show how the construction of *Hobson's Choice* contributes to its overall dramatic effect.

Hobson's Choice is a traditional comedy which owes much to the conventions of the 'well-made play'. Brighouse's craftsmanlike, pragmatic approach to dramatic construction is shown to perfect effect in this play, and it owes a great deal of its lasting popularity to his meticulous skill.

A swift succession of characters and incidents upon the stage is used to hold the attention of the audience, and this is achieved by the division of each act into 'scenelets' marked by the entrances and exits of the various characters. Brighouse's economic methods allow the essence of a situation to be conveyed in a very short space of time. In the first act, for example, the opening lines prepare us for Hobson's entrance and make us curious to see the man who frightens Albert and who is the subject of his daughters' comments. They also suggest, however, Hobson's vice — since it is after a Masons' meeting that he rises so late — and demonstrate Maggie's strength of character in the encounter with Albert. In this way, Brighouse unobtrusively but effectively prepares us for the main conflicts of the play.

As the first act progresses, further devices increase the dramatic effect of the play. Maggie's silence after her father calls her 'a proper old maid' and Mrs Hepworth's request that Will is to tell her if he moves from Hobson's means that Maggie's proposal, while dramatic, is not improbable. Dramatic construction also generates humour, especially at the pompous Hobson's expense. From his arrogant lecture to his daughters on uppishness he changes to a servile trader, ridiculously eager to please when Mrs Hepworth enters. He changes again when she leaves, declaring that he will not have her in his shop, only to reverse his attitude within seconds when Jim Heeler enters. Humour is also generated by the construction of the scene in which Maggie and Ada Figgins argue over Will. In this case the conventions of romantic comedy are flouted, with two women fighting for the right to the hand of a single man.

Brighouse succeeds in giving the audience necessary information in a manner which is unobtrusive because of the way he constructs *Hobson's Choice*. Hobson's discussion with Jim about what he should do with his daughters allows us to understand what he is thinking in a realistic way. The one point at which we might be over-aware of Brighouse's determination to further the plot in this way comes at the beginning of Act II, where Vickey says that her father ought to take care of his business instead of spending even more time in the Moonraker's. The audience is being informed that Hobson is going downhill more rapidly now that Maggie and Will have left him, but Vickey's comments to Alice, who we feel would be well aware of the situation, have a slight air of contrivance about them. Elsewhere, however, Brighouse manages successfully to integrate contrivance and coincidence into the plot, as in Act II when Hobson falls into Beenstock's cellar. This is essential for advancing the plot, but Hobson's mishap strikes us as plausible because we have been prepared for it by accounts of his increased drinking. It also perfectly symbolises Hobson's fall in his business and personal life.

Other details of construction help to unify the play and increase its dramatic effect. One of these is Maggie's determination to force her family to accept Will. She tries to achieve this when she insists that her sisters should kiss Will in Act II. This is just one in a series of symbolic gestures of acceptance which she contrives throughout the play. In Act III, where she forces Hobson to eat wedding-cake as well as to shake hands with Will, this device is particularly effective because it prefigures the way in which, very shortly after, Maggie tricks her father into promising the money for marriage-settlements. While these parallels strengthen Maggie's grip on events, the use of Will's business card in Act II reminds us of Mrs Hepworth offering her visiting-card in Act I, when he was timid and 'like a rabbit'. The contrast between the two occasions shows us in a dramatic way how far Will has progressed.

Brighouse allows a year to lapse between Acts III and IV. This makes the character development of Hobson and Will more credible. We have now arrived at a position where Will can defeat Hobson. In the two earlier climaxes of the play, at the end of Act I and Act III, we saw Will argue with Hobson in a purely defensive way, or let Maggie do the talking. In Act IV, Will himself takes the initiative. Brighouse also uses very effectively the folk tale or fairy story device of putting each of the daughters to the test. In this way he demonstrates powerfully how, just as Maggie had previously been the most practical of the three, she is also the most compassionate.

Brighouse's construction of *Hobson's Choice* contributes greatly to its dramatic effectiveness and, despite using the familiar devices of naturalistic drama and the 'well-made play', he is able to give them new life with his craftsmanship.

Questions for further study

(1)   Discuss Brighouse's relationship to the theatre of his time.

(2)   How does *Hobson's Choice* reflect the aims of the Repertory Movement and of regional drama?

(3)   Discuss the influence of the Temperance Movement on Brighouse's treatment of the subject of drink in *Hobson's Choice*.

(4)   Discuss *Hobson's Choice* as a treatment of the position of women in society.

(5)   Discuss the significance of the title *Hobson's Choice*.

(6)   Is *Hobson's Choice* anything more than good entertainment?

(7)   Discuss Brighouse's dramatic technique in *Hobson's Choice*.

(8)   Examine the relationship between the attitudes towards work and class in *Hobson's Choice*.

(9)   Does character matter more than plot in *Hobson's Choice*?

(10) Discuss the various means by which *Hobson's Choice* achieves its comic effects.

Part 5

Suggestions for
further reading

DESPITE the popularity of *Hobson's Choice* the play has attracted little critical notice. Material which would prove useful to students of drama as well as of English literature is listed below.

Some of the original material included in this book is based upon suggestions and information provided by Dr Paul Mortimer. Dr Mortimer has kindly agreed to extend his aid to students using this book, and will answer requests for information from groups or classes of students who write to him. Please enclose a stamped addressed envelope with your letter, which you should send to: Dr Paul Mortimer, Deputy Headmaster, Broad Oak High School, Hazel Avenue, Bury, Lancashire, England, BL9 7QT.

The text

BRIGHOUSE, H.: *Hobson's Choice*, Heinemann Educational Books, London, 1964, reprinted 1986 (twice), 1987. This has a good, if slightly outdated introduction by E.R. Wood.

BRIGHOUSE, H.: Manuscript of *Hobson's Choice*. This shows several minor changes to the published version and has some additional closing lines. It can be consulted at Salford Local History Library, Peel Park, Salford, England.

Other works by Brighouse

BRIGHOUSE, H.: *What I Have Had*, Harrap, London, 1953. Brighouse's autobiography is indispensable to any study of his life and times.

BRIGHOUSE, H.: *The Manchester Drama*, Sherratt and Hughes, Manchester, 1917. This deals mainly with other members of the Manchester School of dramatists.

Works on Brighouse

HOWE, P.P.: *The Repertory Theatre: a record and a criticism*, Secker and Warburg, London, 1910. This outlines the origins of the Repertory Movement.

PAYNE, B.I.: *A Life in a Wooden O: memoirs of the theatre*, Yale University

Press, New Haven, Connecticut, 1977. This gives an account of the first production of *Hobson's Choice*.

POWELL, G. and JACKSON, A.: *The Repertory Movement: a history of regional theatre in Britain*, Cambridge University Press, Cambridge, 1984. A good, balanced account.

PRATT, T.: *The Manchester Dramatists*, Sherratt and Hughes, Manchester, 1914. This includes a chapter on Brighouse.

VINSON, J. (ED.): *Contemporary Dramatists*, St James Press, London, 1977. This includes a brief biography of Brighouse.

In addition to these publications, students may wish to obtain programmes from theatres which have produced *Hobson's Choice* or other plays by Brighouse and may still have copies. Here are three of the most recent:

Royal Exchange Theatre, Manchester: *Zack* produced in 1986.

Leeds Playhouse, Leeds: *Hobson's Choice* produced in 1987.

Bolton Octagon Theatre: *Hobson's Choice* produced in 1987.

The author of these notes

JOHN GOODBY is a graduate of the University of Hull (BA) and of the University of Leeds (PhD). He is currently a holder of a Yorkshire Arts Council Writer's Bursary, and is working on a book dealing with contemporary Irish poetry for Manchester University Press's Cultural Politics series. He is presently Tutor of English at Harrogate Tutorial College, England.

York Notes: list of titles

CHINUA ACHEBE
A Man of the People
Arrow of God
Things Fall Apart

EDWARD ALBEE
Who's Afraid of Virginia Woolf?

ELECHI AMADI
The Concubine

ANONYMOUS
Beowulf
Everyman

JOHN ARDEN
Serjeant Musgrave's Dance

AYI KWEI ARMAH
The Beautiful Ones Are Not Yet Born

W. H. AUDEN
Selected Poems

JANE AUSTEN
Emma
Mansfield Park
Northanger Abbey
Persuasion
Pride and Prejudice
Sense and Sensibility

HONORÉ DE BALZAC
Le Père Goriot

SAMUEL BECKETT
Waiting for Godot

SAUL BELLOW
Henderson, The Rain King

ARNOLD BENNETT
Anna of the Five Towns

WILLIAM BLAKE
Songs of Innocence, Songs of Experience

ROBERT BOLT
A Man For All Seasons

ANNE BRONTË
The Tenant of Wildfell Hall

CHARLOTTE BRONTË
Jane Eyre

EMILY BRONTË
Wuthering Heights

ROBERT BROWNING
Men and Women

JOHN BUCHAN
The Thirty-Nine Steps

JOHN BUNYAN
The Pilgrim's Progress

BYRON
Selected Poems

ALBERT CAMUS
L'Etranger (The Outsider)

GEOFFREY CHAUCER
Prologue to the Canterbury Tales
The Clerk's Tale
The Franklin's Tale
The Knight's Tale
The Merchant's Tale
The Miller's Tale
The Nun's Priest's Tale
The Pardoner's Tale
The Wife of Bath's Tale
Troilus and Criseyde

ANTON CHEKOV
The Cherry Orchard

SAMUEL TAYLOR COLERIDGE
Selected Poems

WILKIE COLLINS
The Moonstone
The Woman in White

SIR ARTHUR CONAN DOYLE
The Hound of the Baskervilles

WILLIAM CONGREVE
The Way of the World

JOSEPH CONRAD
Heart of Darkness
Lord Jim
Nostromo
The Secret Agent
Victory
Youth and *Typhoon*

STEPHEN CRANE
The Red Badge of Courage

BRUCE DAWE
Selected Poems

WALTER DE LA MARE
Selected Poems

DANIEL DEFOE
A Journal of the Plague Year
Moll Flanders
Robinson Crusoe

CHARLES DICKENS
A Tale of Two Cities
Bleak House
David Copperfield
Dombey and Son
Great Expectations
Hard Times
Little Dorrit
Nicholas Nickleby
Oliver Twist
Our Mutual Friend
The Pickwick Papers

EMILY DICKINSON
Selected Poems

JOHN DONNE
Selected Poems

THEODORE DREISER
Sister Carrie

GEORGE ELIOT
Adam Bede
Middlemarch
Silas Marner
The Mill on the Floss

T. S. ELIOT
Four Quartets
Murder in the Cathedral
Selected Poems
The Cocktail Party
The Waste Land

J. G. FARRELL
The Siege of Krishnapur

GEORGE FARQUHAR
The Beaux Stratagem

WILLIAM FAULKNER
Absalom, Absalom!
As I Lay Dying
Go Down, Moses
The Sound and the Fury

HENRY FIELDING
Joseph Andrews
Tom Jones

F. SCOTT FITZGERALD
Tender is the Night
The Great Gatsby

JOHN OSBORNE
Look Back in Anger
WILFRED OWEN
Selected Poems
ALAN PATON
Cry, The Beloved Country
THOMAS LOVE PEACOCK
Nightmare Abbey and *Crotchet Castle*
HAROLD PINTER
The Birthday Party
The Caretaker
PLATO
The Republic
ALEXANDER POPE
Selected Poems
THOMAS PYNCHON
The Crying of Lot 49
SIR WALTER SCOTT
Ivanhoe
Quentin Durward
The Heart of Midlothian
Waverley
PETER SHAFFER
The Royal Hunt of the Sun
WILLIAM SHAKESPEARE
A Midsummer Night's Dream
Antony and Cleopatra
As You Like It
Coriolanus
Cymbeline
Hamlet
Henry IV Part I
Henry IV Part II
Henry V
Julius Caesar
King Lear
Love's Labour Lost
Macbeth
Measure for Measure
Much Ado About Nothing
Othello
Richard II
Richard III
Romeo and Juliet
Sonnets
The Merchant of Venice
The Taming of the Shrew
The Tempest
The Winter's Tale
Troilus and Cressida
Twelfth Night
The Two Gentlemen of Verona
GEORGE BERNARD SHAW
Androcles and the Lion
Arms and the Man
Caesar and Cleopatra
Candida
Major Barbara
Pygmalion
Saint Joan
The Devil's Disciple
MARY SHELLEY
Frankenstein
PERCY BYSSHE SHELLEY
Selected Poems
RICHARD BRINSLEY SHERIDAN
The School for Scandal
The Rivals
WOLE SOYINKA
The Lion and the Jewel
The Road
Three Shorts Plays
EDMUND SPENSER
The Faerie Queene (Book I)

JOHN STEINBECK
Of Mice and Men
The Grapes of Wrath
The Pearl
LAURENCE STERNE
A Sentimental Journey
Tristram Shandy
ROBERT LOUIS STEVENSON
Kidnapped
Treasure Island
Dr Jekyll and Mr Hyde
TOM STOPPARD
Professional Foul
Rosencrantz and Guildenstern are Dead
JONATHAN SWIFT
Gulliver's Travels
JOHN MILLINGTON SYNGE
The Playboy of the Western World
TENNYSON
Selected Poems
W. M. THACKERAY
Vanity Fair
DYLAN THOMAS
Under Milk Wood
EDWARD THOMAS
Selected Poems
FLORA THOMPSON
Lark Rise to Candleford
J. R. R. TOLKIEN
The Hobbit
The Lord of the Rings
CYRIL TOURNEUR
The Revenger's Tragedy
ANTHONY TROLLOPE
Barchester Towers
MARK TWAIN
Huckleberry Finn
Tom Sawyer
JOHN VANBRUGH
The Relapse
VIRGIL
The Aeneid
VOLTAIRE
Candide
EVELYN WAUGH
Decline and Fall
A Handful of Dust
JOHN WEBSTER
The Duchess of Malfi
The White Devil
H. G. WELLS
The History of Mr Polly
The Invisible Man
The War of the Worlds
ARNOLD WESKER
Chips with Everything
Roots
PATRICK WHITE
Voss
OSCAR WILDE
The Importance of Being Earnest
TENNESSEE WILLIAMS
The Glass Menagerie
VIRGINIA WOOLF
Mrs Dalloway
To the Lighthouse
WILLIAM WORDSWORTH
Selected Poems
WILLIAM WYCHERLEY
The Country Wife
W. B. YEATS
Selected Poems

York Handbooks: list of titles

YORK HANDBOOKS form a companion series to York Notes and are designed to meet the wider needs of students of English and related fields. Each volume is a compact study of a given subject area, written by an authority with experience in communicating the essential ideas to students of all levels.